A Day in the Life
of the Brain

Brain Works

A Day in the Life of the Brain

Ana María Rodríguez, Ph.D.

SERIES EDITOR
Eric H. Chudler, Ph.D.

CHELSEA HOUSE
PUBLISHERS
An imprint of Infobase Publishing

A Day in the Life of the Brain

Chelsea House
An imprint of Infobase Publishing
132 West 31st Street
New York NY 10001

Library of Congress Cataloging-in-Publication Data

Rodríguez, Ana María, 1958–
    A day in the life of the brain / Ana María Rodríguez.
      p. cm. — (Brain works)
    Includes bibliographical references and index.
    ISBN 0-7910-8947-9 (hardcover)
    1. Brain—Juvenile literature. 2. Thought and thinking—Juvenile literature. I. Title.
    II. Series.
    QP376.R58 2006
    612.8'2--dc22   2006010970

Chelsea House books are available at special discounts when purchased in bulk quantities for businesses, associations, institutions, or sales promotions. Please call our Special Sales Department in New York at (212) 967-8800 or (800) 322-8755.

You can find Chelsea House on the World Wide Web at http://www.chelseahouse.com

Text design by Keith Trego
Cover design by Takeshi Takahashi

Printed in the United States of America

Bang KT 10 9 8 7 6 5 4 3 2 1

This book is printed on acid-free paper.

All links and Web addresses were checked and verified to be correct at the time of publication. Because of the dynamic nature of the Web, some addresses and links may have changed since publication and may no longer be valid.

Table of Contents

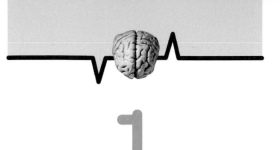

1

Welcome to Mark's Brain

Mark had it all planned. He had control of the soccer ball and there was a clear path toward the goal through the center of the defense. He would sprint straight ahead, keeping the ball close, fake left, then kick the ball into the upper right corner of the goal. It was a simple plan, and he was sure it would work. It had worked before.

But two defenders from the other team approached him quickly from his left side. In a split second, the situation changed and Mark's plan to score a goal was no longer an option. As the defenders got closer, Mark was forced to deviate from a straight line to a diagonal path toward the right corner of the goal box. In a fraction of a moment, he had to construct a "plan B" if he wanted to score a goal.

Running at maximum speed, Mark approached the goal from the right side. It would not be an easy shot, but he had to take it now. He kicked the ball as hard as he could. The ball followed a curved path in the air and soared into the goal at the upper left corner. As Mark kicked the ball, his body leaned to the side and he almost fell to the ground. But, he managed to quickly regain his balance. He had scored a goal! Mark couldn't believe it! With a smile on his face, he gave a high-five to his teammates. All this had happened in less than 10 seconds.

"How did you do it?" asked his teammates. "I don't know," Mark said, "I just did." The answer to their question lies inside Mark's head. He did it thanks to a soft, rounded, grayish-pink organ with a wrinkled surface and a spongy texture. The organ weighs approximately 3 pounds (1.4 kilograms) when fully grown. It is the most complex organ inside Mark's body. Welcome to Mark's brain!

IT'S ALL IN MARK'S HEAD

The **brain** may be visually unappealing, but it is nevertheless, a fascinating organ. The brain, protected by a shield of bones (Mark's skull), is what allowed Mark to coordinate numerous body movements that happily ended in a goal for his team.

Mark had been watching the location of the ball on the soccer field as well as the locations of his teammates and the opposing players. He called for the ball as soon as he saw an opening in the center of the field. He secured the ball with his foot and headed for the goal. All these activities—watching the game, calling for the ball, controlling the ball, and planning a strategy to score a goal—were coordinated by his brain.

Mark's brain received visual information from his eyes, which was used to make the decision to ask his teammates for the ball. His brain coordinated the visual image of the ball coming toward him, trapping the ball with his foot, and then dribbling the ball toward the goal. In his brain, Mark made the decision for a straight approach to the goal. He knew this strategy might work because he had memories stored in his brain of it working before. But as soon as the two defenders came to intercept the ball, the situation changed and Mark had to come up with a different strategy, using his brain, of course.

One of the most fascinating and amazing facts about the brain is that it works at astonishing speeds. The brain communicates with the rest of the body by sending and receiving messages that travel at different speeds depending on which path they take. They can go as fast as 260 miles per hour (approximately 420 kilometers per hour), which is faster than a Formula One race car. In Mark's situation, it was critical for his body to communicate with his brain at these amazing speeds. The two approaching defenders put Mark in an emergency situation that called for fast action. Mark's brain put together the information it received through his eyes about the locations of the defenders and the distance to the goal. It was his brain that coordinated his leg movements and the power of his kick. His brain also perceived that he was about to fall and sent the necessary brain signals at racing speed to the muscles in his body to regain balance. When Mark felt happy about scoring a goal, his brain processed this emotion and sent a signal to his face muscles to produce a smile.

THE BRAIN'S BIG JOB

Mark's brain has a big job. It takes care of all of Mark's body functions, whether he is aware of them or not. Mark's heart beats without stopping, his lungs breathe, and his stomach digests food thanks to his brain, which continuously monitors and controls these activities and more. Mark does not have to worry about taking care of these vital body functions—his brain does it automatically and independently from his will.

Mark picks up a pencil to do his homework, scratches an itchy spot behind his ear, and tastes salty popcorn using his brain. Mark's creative side is also possible because of his brain. He can play the piano, draw a picture, and come up with a plan to surprise his best friend for his birthday. Mark's brain allows him to coordinate all the necessary ideas and activities involved in this process.

In his brain, Mark stores all his memories, good and bad, and his brain recalls these memories the next time a similar smell or sound reminds him of them. He uses memories of past experiences to make decisions about future actions. If Mark gets hurt after jumping into a pool from the shallow side, his brain will learn the hard way to associate jumping and the shallow end of a pool with the pain he felt the first time. The next time he goes to the pool, Mark will be sure to jump into the deep end. In a similar way, Mark's brain stores pleasant experiences in his memory. The first time he tried chocolate ice cream, his favorite flavor, he enjoyed it so much that his brain remembered the sensation and made his mouth water the next time he entered the ice cream shop.

Mark uses his brain to learn what teachers teach him in school, to ride a bike, and to play video games. Mark can read a book, write his homework, whistle a tune, and talk to his friends because of his brain. Mark's brain also processes all his emotions: he feels happy after scoring a goal, gets nervous before a test, or is angry when somebody cheats. His brain wakes him in the morning and makes him go to sleep and dream at night.

Mark is the kind of person he is because of his brain. His brain puts together all his experiences, memories, likes and dislikes, fears, wishes, abilities, feelings, personality, and ambitions to create a unique individual. Just like Mark, you are also a unique individual. No one shares your exact same experiences, knowledge, memories, abilities, or any other traits that make you who you are. And you have your brain to thank for it.

MAKING THE CONNECTIONS

To take care of its big job, Mark's brain communicates with the rest of the body through two important connections. The first one is the **spinal cord**, which looks like a rope that runs down along the center of the back from the base of the brain to the lower back. It is protected by a bony canal called the **spinal column**. The spinal cord is made of a bundle of special fibers called **nerves** enveloped in three layers of membranes called the **meninges**. The spinal cord and the brain together form the **central nervous system**, the most protected and complex system in Mark's body (Figure 1.1).

The second connection that links the brain with the body is another set of nerves called the **peripheral nervous system**. This network of nerves branches out from the spinal cord and brain in a way similar to branches projecting out from a tree trunk. Peripheral nerves connect Mark's central nervous system with each and every part of his body.

Through the peripheral nervous system, the brain receives messages carried by **sensory nerves** coming from all parts of the body. Messages carried by sensory nerves inform the brain what activity the body is performing or sensing. For example, nerves coming from the eyes will tell the brain that the defenders are approaching Mark from his left side. The brain sends messages back to his legs through **motor nerves**. The messages transmitted through motor nerves

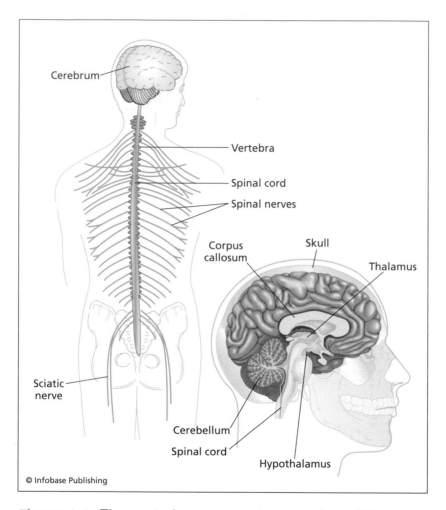

Cerebrum

Vertebra

Spinal cord

Spinal nerves

Corpus
callosum

Skull

Thalamus

Sciatic
nerve

Cerebellum

Spinal cord

Hypothalamus

© Infobase Publishing

Figure 1.1 **The central nervous system consists of the brain and spinal cord. The spinal nerves and other nerves throughout the body make up the peripheral nervous system.**

carry instructions about what to do next. In this case, Mark quickly changed his path to the right side of the goal, away from the defenders. Then, when Mark saw the defenders getting closer, he kicked the ball hard with his foot and scored.

Mark's central and peripheral nervous systems function together to keep his body working every minute of his life.

Wiring the Brain

By the time Mark was born, his brain was already formed inside his skull, but it was far from being ready to work like an adult brain. As a newborn baby, Mark could not see very well, he could not recognize many different sounds, and he could not coordinate his body movements. To learn to do all these things and more, Mark's brain had to receive input from the environment. His brain needed the sounds, sights, touch, smells, and tastes around him to guide the neurons in his brain to establish the necessary connections among them and with sensory organs.

Without such input, the brain will not be able to make the correct connections. Scientists know, for example, that if a perfectly good eye in a newborn cat is covered at birth, the cat will never be able to see with that eye after it is uncovered months later. Although there is nothing wrong with the eye, the cat cannot see with it because there are no neurons connecting that eye to the brain. The newborn neurons in the brain needed the light to guide them to establish the eye–brain connection. Because those neurons literally never "saw the light," they were wired to work somewhere else.

The major brain wiring occurs in early childhood, but wiring never really stops. As Mark grows into an adult, he will still be able to wire some parts of his brain. Every time he learns a new skill, physical or mental, neurons in his brain establish new connections and reinforce old connections to help him remember it.

THE BUILDING BLOCKS OF THE BRAIN

Like all the other organs in the body, the brain, the spinal cord, and all the nerves that form the nervous system are made up of building blocks called cells. There are two main types of cells in the nervous system: nerve cells (neurons) and glial cells (glia).

Neurons have a unique shape that is very different from the shape of the other cells in the body, and this shape suits their job perfectly. Neurons have the important job of transmitting signals known as **nerve impulses** throughout the body. The signal moves only in one direction along neurons. It travels from the **cell body** down a long, hair-like extension known as an **axon**. The signal is received by the **dendrites** of the next neuron and continues its path along the axon to the following neuron (Figure 1.2).

The point where a "transmitting" neuron meets a "receiving" neuron is called the **synapse**. Synapses puzzled scientists for years. They knew that synapses were the places where "messages" passed from one neuron to the next, but they could also see, using powerful microscopes, that neurons do not touch each other at synapses. Neurons are very close to each other, but are always separated by a small space called the synaptic cleft. If the cells do not touch each other, how is the nerve signal transmitted? The answer to this puzzle is **neurotransmitters**. Neurotransmitters are chemicals that the transmitting cell releases into the synaptic cleft. They act like messengers binding to the receiving cell and triggering a nerve impulse that travels along the axon, and to the next cell in the same manner.

In addition to neurons, the nervous system also contains **glial cells**, which help neurons do their job. One way glial cells assist neurons is by wrapping themselves around axons

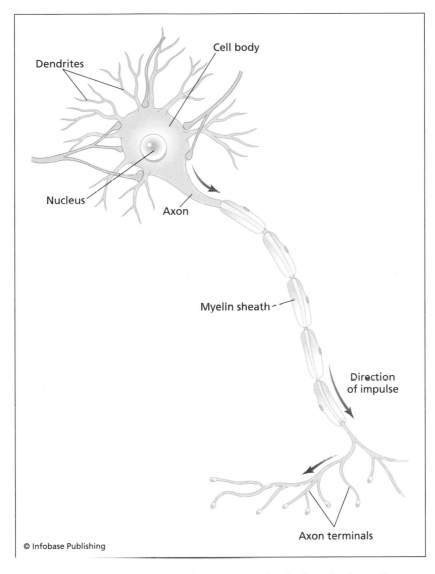

Figure 1.2 **A neuron sends an electrical signal along its axon, which is then received by the dendrites of adjacent neurons.**

of the neuron. This wrapping is called **myelin**. This helps neurons do their job better because axons that are myelinated carry nerve impulses faster than those that are not. Special glial cells called **astrocytes** have another important job. They transport nutrients to neurons and eliminate parts of dead neurons.

THE MAIN PARTS OF THE BRAIN

The brain is the most complex organ in the body, encased by the skull and formed by the **cerebrum**, the **cerebellum**, and the **brain stem**. With just one hand, you could hold a human brain and you would have about 98% of all the neural tissue of the body. There are approximately 100 billion neurons in an adult brain and about 10 times that number of glial cells. If you could actually hold a brain in your hand and look at it from the top, you would see that this complicated organ is divided into a left and a right side, called the left and the right **hemispheres**.

The left and right hemispheres are not always of the same size. Left-handed people usually have symmetric brains, meaning that the left and the right hemispheres are about the same size. Right-handed people tend to have asymmetric brains with the left hemisphere being larger than the right. It appears that the right hemisphere is dominant for spatial abilities, face recognition, creating visual images, and music, while the left hemisphere seems to dominate language, math, and logic. Even though the brain seems to divide main functions between its left and right hemispheres, the two halves are connected and work together.

As strange as it may seem, each hemisphere controls the actions and receives the sensations perceived by the opposite side of the body. For example, your right hemisphere is in charge of moving your left arm and leg, as well as of receiving the sensations originating in your left eye and ear.

Although each hemisphere is in charge of only one side of the body, they work together. The result of this cooperation is that the left and the right sides of your body can perform coordinated movements, such as catching a football with two hands. The right and the left hemisphere can work together because they communicate through a bridge of living tissue called the **corpus callosum**, a large bundle of nerve fibers linking the left and right sides of the brain.

Each of the hemispheres is made up of four **brain lobes** (Figure 1.3). The frontal lobe is located toward the front side of the brain. Its main role involves **executive functions** like reasoning, planning, and problem solving. The frontal lobe is also responsible for speech, movement, and emotions. The parietal lobe is located behind the frontal lobe and its functions include perception of touch, pressure, temperature, and pain. The temporal lobe is located toward the side of the brain (around where the ears are) and its functions involve memory formation and the perception of sounds. The occipital lobe is located toward the back of the brain; this is where vision perception takes place.

The lobes are protrusions separated by **sulci** (fissures) and **gyri** (the twisted bumps on the surface of the brain). The patterns of sulci and gyri are similar in most people, but no two are exactly alike.

THE SENSES: THE BRAIN'S PORTALS TO THE OUTSIDE WORLD

Without his five **senses**, Mark would have a hard time getting through a day. He would even have a hard time getting out of his room! As an experiment, Mark stood in the middle of his room, closed his eyes, plugged his ears, kept his arms to the sides of his body, and spun around twice. Without opening his

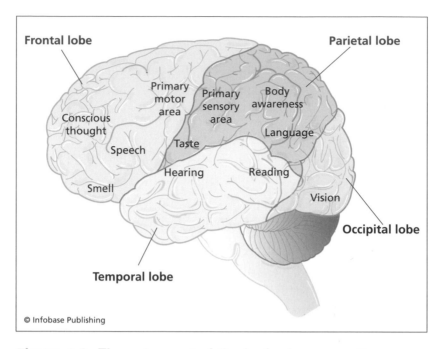

Figure 1.3 **The outer part of the brain, known as the cerebral cortex, is divided into four lobes. The body's functions, such as taste, speech, and hearing, are associated with specific regions within these four lobes.**

eyes or reaching out his arms, he tried to leave his room. He bumped against the bed, tripped on a video game controller, and ran into a wall. He could not leave his room because his brain had no visual or tactile (touch) information to find a clear path to the door. Even if somebody had called his name, his brain could not have guided him to the door by following his or her voice because Mark had plugged his ears and could not hear.

Mark's senses are his brain's portals to the outside world. Mark detects light, color, shapes, movement, and depth with his eyes. He detects a variety of sounds with his sense of hearing and numerous aromas with his sense of smell. He identifies many different flavors with his sense of taste. He can tell apart different shapes, their temperatures, and textures with his sense of touch. His senses detect the outside world—for example, light, heat, or sound sensations—and translate them into the language of the brain, nerve impulses. The brain processes the information about the outside world in the **sensory cortex** and then takes the necessary actions to get Mark through a day, or just to get him out of his room!

To get through a day, Mark performs numerous tasks. He does things on his own, he interacts with other people, and he moves in and out of places. His brain coordinates all these activities, but it does not do it alone. To coordinate all these activities successfully, Mark's brain needs to know what is going on outside the body. Being encased inside the skull, the brain has no direct means to know about the world outside. It needs a portal or gateway and the senses provide it.

To see the brain in action, let us follow Mark through what began as an uneventful day, but ended up having a couple of twists and turns.

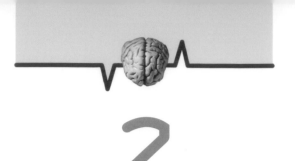

2

Rise and Shine

Loud music blared out of Mark's radio alarm clock, filling his room. It was time to wake up and get ready for school. Mark sat on his bed and rubbed his eyes while his brain switched from sleeping mode to waking mode. Switching the brain from sleeping to waking is one job of Mark's **hypothalamus** (Figure 2.1). The hypothalamus regulates Mark's "internal clock," which makes him go to sleep at night and wake up in the morning. Mark's hypothalamus regulates the waking and sleeping periods by adjusting the levels of a hormone or body chemical called **melatonin**.

Now that Mark's brain has switched to the waking mode, he hears the music clearly. His ears detect the sound waves coming from the radio and transmit them from the outer ears on the sides

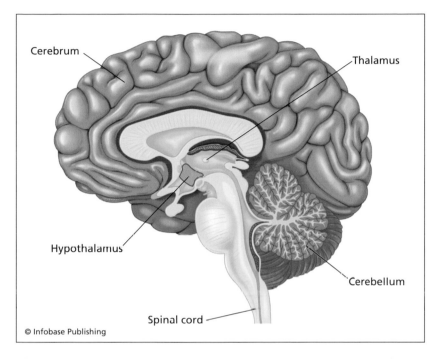

Cerebrum

Thalamus

Hypothalamus

Cerebellum

Spinal cord

© Infobase Publishing

Figure 2.1 **The hypothalamus regulates the sleep cycle and also helps the body cope with stress. The thalamus acts as a relay station for much of the information that passes through the brain.**

of his head through the auditory canal inside his head. Inside the auditory canal, sound waves are converted to mechanical vibrations by the ear drum. The ear drum moves tiny bones in the middle ear that then stimulate receptor cells in the inner ear. The receptor cells convert the vibrations to nerve impulses and send them to the brain.

HEARING AND SMELLING

Mark is now aware of the music and even recognizes the song when the nerve impulses reach a part of his brain called

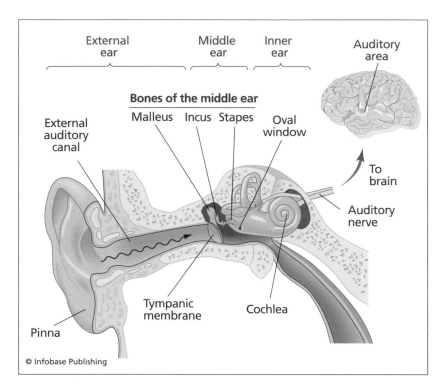

Figure 2.2 **The human ear converts sound waves into electrical impulses. These impulses travel down the auditory nerve to the auditory cortex (area) of the brain.**

the **auditory cortex** (Figure 2.2). This area is located on the outside part of his brain, just above the ears.

Mark is also aware of other sounds, such as the noises his mom makes while she cooks breakfast in the kitchen. His other senses provide more information about his surroundings. He can now detect the smell of toast coming from the kitchen. The heat from the toaster releases invisible particles from the bread as it toasts. These airborne particles carry the smell to Mark's nose. In his nose, the hairs and mucus trap the particles and trigger nerve impulses in the olfactory

nerve. This nerve, which links the nose to the brain, carries
the scent sensations directly to the **olfactory cortex** in the

Smelling Disorders

Aah! The smells of pizza and freshly baked cookies are wonderful.
They not only stimulate your appetite, but also make you happy.
Have you ever wondered how your life would change if you could
not smell anything?

Scientists have estimated that approximately 14 million
Americans have problems or disorders with their sense of smell.
There are different kinds of smelling disorders and they have
intriguing names. For example, people who have completely
lost their ability to smell have anosmia. People who perceive
harmless or pleasant smells as offensive have parosmia, and
those who smell things that are not there have phantosmia.

One of the main consequences of losing the ability to smell
is that the sense of taste is lost too. Although smell and taste
are separate senses, each with their own receptors and areas in
the cortex, taste is permanently linked to smell. Dr. Alan Hirsh,
a neurologist with the Smell and Taste Research Institute in
Chicago, says that when his patients go to Thanksgiving dinner,
"they can't smell the scents of cooking and everything tastes
like Styrofoam." Not being able to smell and taste food makes
these patients sad, because smell and taste connect with the
amygdala, located in the emotional center of the brain.

Not being able to smell has more consequences. For example,
people with anosmia are not able to tell if food is bad to eat or
if it is burning on the stove. People might suffer from a smell
disorder after having a nasal infection, a serious head injury, a
tumor, or surgery.

brain. The olfactory cortex is also part of the cortex, located on both hemispheres in an area approximately above the eyes (the temporal lobe).

The neurons in the olfactory cortex process the smell sensation and Mark then recognizes it as the smell of toast. Mark feels happy anticipating eating his favorite breakfast. The smell of toast triggers another memory in Mark's brain—it is a weekday and he has to eat breakfast and go to school.

TASTING BREAKFAST

Sitting at the kitchen table, Mark spreads butter and grape jelly over his toast and takes a big bite. A variety of sensations fill his mouth as he tastes the sweet jelly and the buttery flavors. He also detects sensations such as the crunchy bread crust, the stickiness of the jelly, and the slippery feeling of the butter. He is able to detect all these different sensations with the **papillae** that cover his mouth and his tongue.

The papillae look like tiny bumps located on the surface of the tongue and on the inside of his mouth. Mark differentiates between the different flavors and textures using various types of papillae. Each papilla has a gustatory nerve that transmits the sensation from the papilla to the brain region for taste, called the **gustatory cortex**. This region is in both hemispheres on the temporal lobe, just above the olfactory cortex.

When Mark drinks his cold orange juice and his warm cocoa, the papillae respond to the temperature of the liquids and trigger impulses on the nerves that connect them to the brain. These receptors are very useful to Mark because they allow him to combine flavor and texture sensations with the temperature of his toast and drinks.

Besides taste receptors, Mark has pain receptors on his tongue, lips, skin, and inside his mouth. If the cocoa he is

Cool Facts About the Senses of Smell and Taste

◆ Smell is the first bond between baby and mother.

◆ People are capable of recognizing as many as 10,000 different smells.

◆ Smell receptors are replaced about every 30 days with new ones. Only smell and taste receptors are regenerated. The other senses do not have the ability to replace old receptors.

◆ The sense of smell has a powerful effect on your memory. When you smell something it often brings back memories associated with that smell. This happens because the olfactory nerves transmit signals to brain areas involved in memory, like the hippocampus.

◆ People have about 10,000 taste buds distributed on the tongue, inside the cheeks, on the roof of the mouth, and on the throat. By comparison, chickens have about 24 taste buds (so they would eat almost anything you feed them). Catfish, on the other hand, have about 175,000 taste buds. Most of them are outside of their bodies, so they can taste food without even opening their mouths.

◆ Taste receptors are replaced about every 10 days with new receptors. The new ones replace receptors damaged by very hot or cold liquids, harsh spices, and the scrapping action of teeth and hard foods. If Mark burns his tongue with hot chocolate, he will lose his sense of taste only temporarily. As soon as the newly built receptors replace the burnt ones, he will recover his sense of taste.

drinking was too hot, the pain receptors in his lips, tongue, and mouth would have quickly sent the message to the brain. The brain would have recognized it as a dangerous situation and immediately sent the message to Mark to stop drinking and move the cup of hot chocolate away from his mouth. If his ability to feel pain were damaged, Mark could seriously burn his mouth without realizing it.

DOING MORE THAN ONE THING AT A TIME

After breakfast, Mark rides his bike to school. He is not aware of it, but it is his brain that allows him to ride his bike and at the same time, think about what he will talk about with his friends at school.

Riding a bike has become almost an automatic activity: Mark does not have to think about moving the pedals with his feet and keeping his balance. He does not have to give his full attention to riding the bike because his brain has already learned what to do. Furthermore, Mark's brain has stored this knowledge as a permanent memory.

The first time Mark tried to ride his bike, his brain did not know how hard to push the pedals or how to position his body to maintain its balance. But after hours of practice, Mark's brain learned the appropriate body movements. Mark's cerebellum helped him detect when his body was off balance. The cerebellum worked with the visual cortex and the **motor cortex** to correct his body position and movement of his legs and arms until he regained his balance (Figure 2.3).

The more Mark practiced, the better he got. Once he identified the movements and body position that would allow him to stay balanced and ride a bike smoothly, Mark repeated them numerous times. This repetition stimulated his brain to

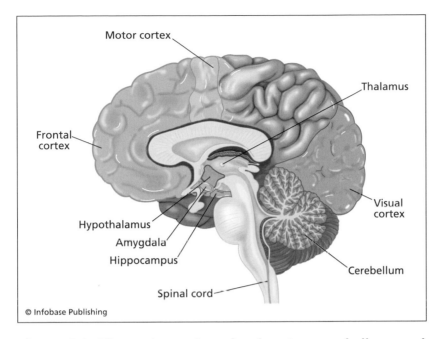

© Infobase Publishing

Figure 2.3 The motor cortex, visual cortex, cerebellum, and hippocampus are responsible for balance and movement.

store the information as a long-term memory with the help of the **hippocampus**. Now, every time Mark gets on his bike, his brain remembers what it learned after hours of practice and does not need to learn it again.

Mark's permanent memories are not stored in a particular region of his brain. At first, scientists thought that there was a special place in the brain for memories. They thought that the brain might store memories just like computers store information in files on different computer drives. But now scientists know that this is not true. In Mark's brain, the memory of a pepperoni pizza, for example, is a combination of information provided by the various senses. When Mark pictures a pepperoni pizza in his mind, his brain combines the sight, smell, taste, and touch sensations of the pizza into one. Mark's brain puts together the images of a pizza covered with white cheese, round slices of pepperoni, and red tomato sauce, with the smell and taste of the pizza and the way it feels in his hands and mouth.

During his ride to school, Mark thinks about the day ahead. For this, he uses the **frontal cortex**, the brain region located behind his forehead. This important brain region is dedicated to high levels of thinking, such as planning activities and coming up with strategies to solve problems. Mark arrives at school on time and prepares for what he expects will be an uneventful day.

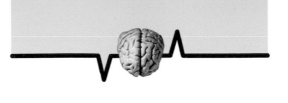

3

Mark's Thinking Side

The school bell rang as Mark entered the building through the main door. He hurried to his first class because he did not want to get a tardy note. His first class was math, which he enjoyed. He liked learning ways to solve everyday problems, such as knowing exactly how much change he would get at the store. His mother let him keep the change, so Mark always wanted to know how much he would get to keep for himself.

Today, Ms. Einstein, the math teacher, gave her class a worksheet with two types of problems. For the first half of the problems, Mark had to calculate the exact result of adding and multiplying single-digit numbers. For the second half, he would have to estimate the result of adding and subtracting single-digit numbers.

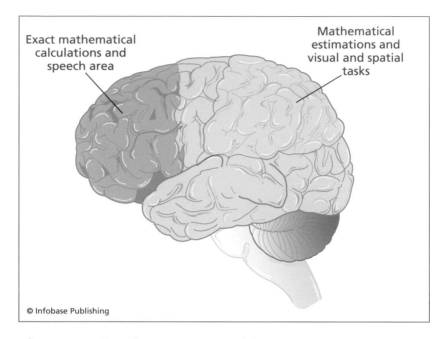

Exact mathematical calculations and speech area

Mathematical estimations and visual and spatial tasks

© Infobase Publishing

Figure 3.1 **The frontal lobe (*red*) is involved with mathematical problems that require exact results. The parietal lobe (*blue*), however, is used if the math involved only requires an estimate as an answer.**

If you could see inside Mark's brain, you would see that he uses different areas of his brain to do exact calculations and estimations. Mark uses left frontal cortex areas when he calculates exact results. However, he uses his left and right parietal cortices when he estimates the answers (Figure 3.1).

Scientists do not know exactly why the brain approaches math this way, but they think that it may have to do with the "tools" the brain needs to do exact calculations versus estimations. The left frontal cortex, which Mark uses to do exact calculations, is the same brain area Mark uses to speak. Scientists think that the brain uses language or specific words, such as the names of the numbers, to calculate an exact mathematical result.

On the other hand, estimation takes place in the **parietal cortex** on both the left and right hemispheres, which are also involved in visual and spatial tasks. So, Mark's brain seems to need visual clues, but not words, to have an idea of how big or small numbers are in order to estimate a result.

Mark finished his math worksheet, gave it to Ms. Einstein, and left for his next class, English.

HOW MARK'S BRAIN HANDLES LANGUAGE

English class filled quickly and Ms. Twain, the English teacher, promptly passed out a reading and writing assignment. Mark had to read a short story and then answer a few questions about it. Ms. Twain always chose fun stories to read, so Mark began immediately.

As Mark read and understood the story, an area in his brain called **Wernicke's area** became very active. When he began writing the answers, a different brain area, **Broca's area**, increased its activity. When the class finished writing the assignment, Ms. Twain asked Mark to read his answers aloud. As Mark spoke, his Broca's area became active again. Broca's area and Wernicke's area are separate from each other, but they communicate through nerve fibers. The two areas work together when Mark listens to or reads a story, and when he talks about it. In the majority of people—about 97%—the Broca's and Wernicke's areas are only found in the left hemisphere of the brain.

The "language" areas in Mark's brain work very closely with his hearing and vision areas. They allow him to see and hear words, understand them, and produce speech. Mark is also able to move his mouth to speak and stand up to answer questions thanks to the motor cortex, which helps coordinate his body movements.

Ms. Twain was pleased with Mark's answers and he felt happy, but soon his mood would change. As Ms. Twain dismissed the class, she reminded them that the talent show would be that afternoon. Mark froze—he had completely

Slurred Speech and "Word Salads"

Language seems to be such a complex activity that the brain has dedicated not one but two distinct areas to handle it. One area handles the processes involved in understanding language, both written and spoken (Wernicke's area). A different area handles the processes related to speaking (Broca's area). So, depending on which area is damaged, a person will have trouble either understanding what others try to tell him or in speaking to others.

When there is damage to Wernicke's area, the person does not understand what others tell him. Since he cannot understand what others are saying, his responses make no sense, even though he says the words correctly. His speech is an incomprehensible mixture of well-spoken words. For example, if somebody asks, "How are you today?" he might answer, "Colors trucks above." Doctors call this way of speaking a "word salad," because the words are all mixed up like vegetables in a salad. On the other hand, when a person has damage to Broca's area, he can understand what others tell him, but when he tries to speak, he does not form words properly and his speech is slow and slurred. To the same question above, he might respond, "I zeel zrine."

forgotten that he had signed up to play his favorite piano piece at the talent show.

FEELING FEAR

Mark realized that he should have practiced the composition a few times the night before to make sure he remembered it, but he had not practiced. What if he forgot the melody in front of everybody?

There was a funny feeling in Mark's stomach. It felt like a sinking sensation or a nervous, fluttering feeling that some people describe as "having butterflies." Mark's palms began to sweat and his mouth felt dry. He was not the only one. Some of his classmates looked worried, too, and probably felt the same way at the thought of appearing on stage and performing in front of a crowd.

Being a little afraid is a normal reaction before performing on stage, before a test, or before competing in a sporting event. Stage fright is the number one fear for most people. They fear it more than death! Mark's reaction to his upcoming performance is called the "fight or flight" response. When Mark knew that the talent show was today, his brain had to decide between facing the situation by stepping up on the stage and performing the best he could ("fight") or trying to avoid the situation by, for example, telling the teacher that he felt sick and could not perform ("flight").

Mark's brain prepares his body for either response, fight or flight, by producing a series of changes in his body automatically. These changes get his body ready for either action. His heart rate increases to pump more blood to his brain and muscles. His lungs breathe faster to provide more oxygen to his body. Mark's senses sharpen—for example, the pupils in

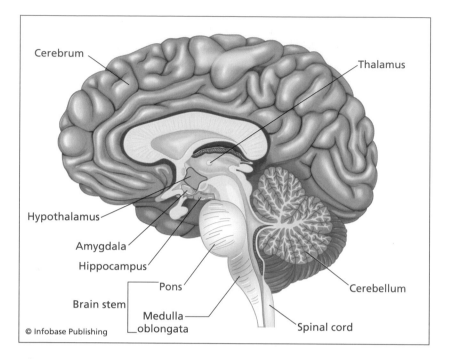

Figure 3.2 **The amygdala and the brain stem work together to produce the "fight or flight" response. Physical changes associated with the response include an increase in heart rate and a tightening of the muscles.**

his eyes get larger to see better and improve his responses—and his concentration also improves. Mark senses changes in his body, such as sweaty hands, increased breathing, and a dry mouth.

The area of Mark's brain that is involved in producing fear is the **amygdala** (Figure 3.2). The amygdala interacts with the brain stem, which is the part of the central nervous system that regulates heartbeat, breathing, and other vital body functions. The amygdala sends a message to the brain stem to increase breathing and the heartbeat. It also stimulates the areas that control sensory perceptions to enhance them. All these reactions involve the autonomic nervous system. The "fight or flight" response is temporary and will go away soon after Mark decides what to do.

But what will Mark do? Will he conquer his fear and play his favorite piano piece in front of the audience? His sharpened senses and concentration will make it easier for him to remember the music. He already knows how to play the piece, but wishes he had practiced the night before to refresh his memory. Or will Mark take "flight" from his performance, letting the butterflies in his stomach and his racing heart stop him from playing?

Birdsongs and Learning a Second Language

Kids and Zebra finches have something in common: kids learn a language the same way that birds learn their songs. Kids and birds must be able to hear an adult speak or sing, and they should be able to hear themselves as they imitate the adult sounds. Being able to hear the words (or having auditory feedback) is so important to developing and maintaining speech that when children lose their hearing, they gradually lose their ability to form words properly.

It seems that the same strategy applies to learning a second language. The more children listen to the radio or to people talking in the second language, and the more they themselves talk in the second language, the more successfully they will

(continues)

(continued)

learn it. Auditory feedback is more helpful than writing or reading the second language.

How does the brain handle a second language? It all depends on how old the person was when he or she learned it. When a young person learns a second language, he or she speaks it using the same region of Broca's area used to speak the first language, and he or she understands it using the same region of Wernicke's area used to understand the first language. However, when adults learn a second language, they train a new region in the Broca's area to speak the new language. This new region is separate from the one used to speak the first language. To understand the second language, they use the same part of Wernicke's area used to understand the first language.

This may explain why it is easier for adults to understand a new language than to speak it. Adults have to train a new region in the Broca's area to learn to speak the new language, and this takes time and practice. But understanding a second language is easier because their brains use an already trained part of Wernicke's area.

4

Mark's Social Side

Mark pushed the door open and stepped outside. He squinted when the bright sunlight hit his eyes. When Mark narrowed his eyes, his pupils constricted automatically to reduce excessive light from entering his cyc. Mark did not have to think about closing his eyes—this reaction was a **reflex**. Mark's involuntary reflexes involve the brain stem. The response is quick to protect the body from harm, such as extremely bright light that might injure the receptors on the back of the eyes.

Mark walked toward the outdoor theatre. He walked up the stairs to reach the stage and met his class for a play rehearsal. They prepared the set by bringing tables, chairs, and other items. They hung posters, then pushed and lifted boxes. All those body

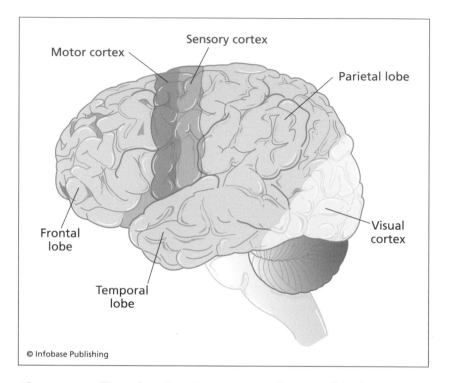

Figure 4.1 **The visual cortex communicates with the motor cortex to guide movement. The sensory cortex, which is responsible for the sense of touch, lies adjacent to the motor cortex.**

movements involved Mark's senses as well as numerous muscles in his body. The motor cortex is the area in Mark's brain that controls voluntary body movements, such as moving his arms and legs, bending over, or turning his head when a friend calls his name.

The sensory cortices, which are the areas in Mark's brain that receive and interpret the information sent by his senses, are connected to the motor cortex (Figure 4.1). This connection allows Mark's brain to receive the sensory information and produce specific body movements. For example, when Mark decides to climb a ladder to hang a poster on the stage, his eyes send information about the distance between the steps to the **visual cortex**. In response, the motor cortex sends information first to the spinal cord and then to his leg muscles to adjust the height of his feet as he climbs.

Mark's visual cortex is located on the back of his head, in the occipital lobe of his brain. Nerves act like wires connecting the visual cortex to the motor cortex, allowing "hand-eye" coordination. The other senses send their perceptions to their corresponding sensory areas on the cortex. These sensory areas also connect to the motor cortex to help Mark coordinate all his body movements. This is how visual images, as well as sound, smell, taste, and touch, guide Mark's body movements during his play rehearsal.

CROSSING OVER

One interesting detail about how the brain controls body movements is that the left side or hemisphere controls the right side of the body, and the right hemisphere directs the movements of the left side of the body. The information to move the right foot, for example, travels through nerves from the motor cortex on the left hemisphere of Mark's brain to the brain stem. In the brain stem, the nerves cross to the right side of the body and extend through the spinal cord until they reach the right foot. Scientists learned this when they noticed that people with an injury in the left motor cortex had problems moving their arms and legs on the right side of the body. Scientists later understood how this happened when they took a closer look at the brain, brain stem, and spinal cord. They saw how the nerves coming from the left hemisphere cross to the right side of the body in the brain stem before reaching the appropriate muscles.

EATING LUNCH AND HAVING A GOOD TIME

Mark heard the bell ring, announcing lunchtime. He joined his classmates in a line and walked toward the cafeteria. Mark's stomach gurgled and his mouth watered. He could smell the other students' lunches and realized how hungry he was. The hypothalamus and the brain stem control Mark's appetite (Figure 4.2). These brain areas tell Mark that it is

Chocolate and Your Brain

Mark looked at his lunch spread before him and reached for the chocolate bar. Forget the other foods—his body craved the chocolate bar he had packed. Mark unwrapped the rectangular piece of solid milk chocolate and chewed it slowly, savoring each bite.

What is in chocolate that makes people feel better after they eat it? In the United States, each person eats an average of 11 pounds of chocolate each year. Scientists think that people crave chocolate because some of its ingredients act on the brain, triggering positive moods.

Chocolate has about 380 known chemicals. Scientists have not figured out yet what effect each of the chemicals has on the brain, but they know what some of them do. The caffeine in chocolate acts on the brain to raise people's spirits, make them feel happier, and speed up their hearts. Other chocolate components make the brain release natural opiates, which are brain-made substances that relax the body and dull pain.

time to eat by sending signals to his stomach that stimulate secretions and movements. His brain makes his mouth water, producing more saliva than normal, just like his mouth would do when chewing on food. It is as if his body, anticipating that Mark will eat lunch soon, begins the process of digestion ahead of time.

During lunch, Mark has the opportunity to socialize with his friends. Using his eyes, he searches the crowd of students in the cafeteria until he finds his two best friends. Mark is able to identify their faces thanks to the brain area located in the lower temporal cortex. He can also tell if his friends are

One of these brain-made opiates is called anandamide. Anandamide works in a way similar to how the illegal drug marijuana works in the brain. However, anandamide is made in the brain and does not harm the nervous system like marijuana. The brain produces anandamide in very small amounts that break down quickly. Marijuana has a longer-lasting effect and may damage the brain. Mark could never eat enough chocolate to produce dangerous levels of anandamide in his brain. Chocolate also has phenylethylamine, which increases blood pressure and blood-sugar levels. This makes Mark feel alert and content.

When Mark ate all these substances and others in the chocolate bar, he felt more relaxed and satisfied. Chocolate seems to be good for Mark, but it is not all good news. He knows that chocolate is not the healthiest food because it is full of sugar and high in calories. But eating a bar once in a while will not hurt him too much.

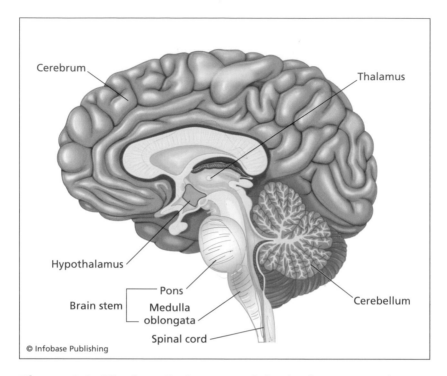

Figure 4.2 **The hypothalamus and the brain stem work together to control appetite.**

happy, worried, sad, or angry by just looking at their faces. Using his lower temporal cortex, Mark has learned to match facial expressions with specific feelings using previous experiences. His brain stores this information with the help of the hippocampus. Mark identifies his friends' emotions using the amygdala.

Mark and his friends sit together and eat lunch. They talk and laugh and have a good time. Laughing is so natural to people that few realize that it involves many muscles in the body. About 13 muscles in Mark's face, lips, jaw, and throat move when he laughs. When laughing a hearty laugh, Mark also uses muscles in his abdomen and chest. A good laugh involves Mark's motor cortex and also a small area in his frontal cortex.

The conversation is lively and Mark feels happy until someone asks, "So, Mark, what are you going to do in the talent show?" The question triggers the unsettling thought of his piano performance. "I'm supposed to play the piano, but I forgot to practice last night," Mark says, lowering his eyes. He suddenly felt the "fight or flight" sensation again, and he was no longer hungry. The bell rang. Lunch was over and Mark slowly walked to his art class.

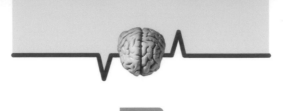

5

Mark's Creative Side

Mr. Velásquez, the art teacher, had all the materials set up for the day's activity. There was a bowl containing a ball of wet, gray clay, another one filled with water, and a plastic apron for each student. Mark tied his blue apron around his waist and neck and sat on his chair. He looked at the blackboard for instructions. Mr. Velásquez wanted the students to use the clay to create an oval plate about the size of a hand.

FEELING COLD

Mark submerged his hands in the bowl of water. The water felt cold. Mark feels how hot or cold objects are because he has special receptors in his skin that can perceive changes in temperature.

Different sets of receptors sense hot and cold temperatures. One set of receptors sends an electric signal to the brain when the temperature is cold. A separate set of receptors signals the brain when the temperature is warm or hot. Although each set senses different temperatures, both sets are of the same type called free nerve ending receptors. Scientists are not sure about how these receptors work exactly. They have evidence that the changes in temperature cause the receptors to change their shape. This change in shape may lead to the production of an electric signal.

The signal produced by temperature receptors in Mark's hands travels through sensory nerves to the spinal cord, crosses the thalamus, and then continues toward the sensory cortex on the brain. In a fraction of a second, Mark knows the water is cold. Mark moved his hands to the other bowl containing the lump of clay. He dug his wet fingers into the wet clay and felt that it, too, was cold.

SENSITIVE FEELINGS

Using his sense of touch, Mark felt that the clay was soft, slippery, and sticky. Mark's hands, especially his fingertips, are one of the body's areas best equipped to perceive how things feel to the touch. Mark has numerous touch receptors buried in his skin and the number of touch receptors is much higher in his fingertips and lips than they are on the palms of his hands. The more numerous the receptors are, the more touch sensations Mark can discriminate.

Touch is different from the other senses in that there is no single organ dedicated to it. There are eyes for vision and ears for hearing, but minute touch receptors are not located in one place. They are within Mark's skin all over his body, and they

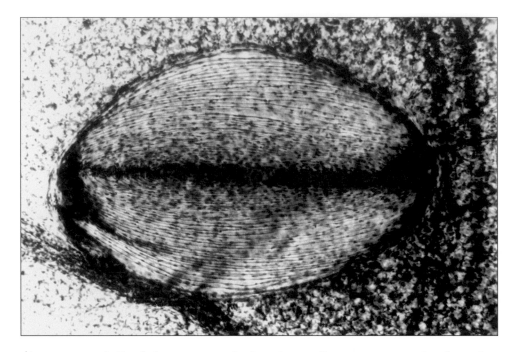

Figure 5.1 **A Pacinian corpuscle is a type of sensory receptor found in the skin and elsewhere in the body. When squeezed or made to change shape, the corpuscle produces a nerve impulse.**

respond to many different amounts of pressure. Some touch receptors are very close to the surface of the skin and they can feel even the light pressure of a mosquito landing on his arm. Other touch receptors surround the roots of hairs on Mark's arms. These receptors are stimulated by the movement of the hairs, such as when a soft breeze blows over his arms.

As Mark's fingers work the clay, the touch receptors in his fingers and hands send electric signals to his spinal cord (Figure 5.1). On their way to the brain, touch sensations cross over when they reach the brain stem. So, what Mark feels on the left side of his body, like a mosquito tickling his left arm, is processed on the right side of his brain. As with Mark's other senses, except smell, the signals continue their route to

Growing Up Without the Sense of Touch

"Don't touch anything!" Mark had heard this many times from his parents when they were visiting a store or a museum. It is not just Mark who feels compelled to explore his surroundings with his hands. All kids reach out to touch or hold in their hands objects that capture their interest. Touch offers a direct means to explore the world around you. It is one of the first senses to develop.

Scientists have discovered that if babies are not held and caressed often, their bodies will not grow as much and their brains will not develop normally. One way scientists discovered this was by studying premature babies. A baby is premature when he or she is born before the usual nine months of growth inside the mother's body. Premature babies are not ready to go home because not all of their organs are fully developed. While their organs finish maturing, the babies must spend all of their time inside an incubator.

When incubators were first used, babies grew smaller than non-premature babies. Their brains also stalled in their development. Scientists discovered that many parts of the babies' brains, not just the one for perceiving touch, were barely active. The only thing these incubator babies lacked was their mother's gentle touch, holding and caressing them many times every day.

So, the doctors had the parents hold their babies, massage them, and care for them as much as possible while they stayed with them in the hospital. In just ten days, the babies receiving caring sessions increased their weight, as well as their brain activity. These babies were also sent home earlier than babies who were not held or massaged.

the brain, passing through the thalamus first and then heading to the sensory cortex.

Mark works the clay with his hands. His delicate sense of touch allows him to feel that the clay is drying, and he pours a bit of water on it. As he shapes his plate, Mark smoothes its sides and edges using his fingertips. He shapes the clay into the desired form, combining touch and visual images. His brain processes these images and coordinates his hand movements using the motor cortex to achieve the desired shape.

OF SHAPES AND COLORS: THE VISUAL WORLD

After working the clay for almost the entire class period, Mark decided that he was happy with his creation. He brought the oval plate to Mr. Velásquez, who put it on a tray with the plates made by Mark's classmates, in order to let them dry.

Now that the students had finished working the clay, Mr. Velásquez asked them to draw a picture of their plate on a white piece of paper. Next, he asked the class to draw a design within the outline of the plate and color it. This would allow them to try a few different designs and color combinations on paper before deciding which design they would draw on the finished plate.

Mark traced a few oval shapes on his paper that represented the plate, and drew different designs within each shape. In one oval shape, he drew a combination of different geometric figures—circles, triangles, squares, and polygons. In another oval, he drew soccer balls because he loved playing the sport. Mark also tried the landscape of a beach in another oval, and finally a cartoon scene from his favorite video game in the last one. He reached for his colored pencils and turned the black-and-white drawings into multicolored images.

As with most of Mark's activities, drawing primarily involves his sense of vision. Vision is one of Mark's best developed senses and the one he relies on most. Mark's eyes are very complex organs. They are capable of focusing light and images. Because Mark has two eyes with intercepting visual ranges, he can also perceive depth. He can tell which objects are closer to him and which are farther away.

Mark's eyes have receptors for color and plain, white light. They can also detect movement. When Mark looks at the colored plates he drew on the paper, receptors in his eyes

Cool Facts About Vision

- ◆ Vision is the sense scientists have studied the most.
- ◆ About one-fourth of the brain is involved in processing visual images, more than for all the other senses.
- ◆ Each eye has about 125 million photoreceptors, cells specialized in turning light into electrical signals.
- ◆ Light receptors come in two types, rods and cones. Rods are most sensitive to dim light (they work better in places with little light) and they do not convey a sense of color. Cones, on the other hand, work in bright light and they transmit acute detail to the brain, as well as information about color.
- ◆ Not all the cones in the eyes perceive the same colors. Some cones are most sensitive to red, others most sensitive to green, and a third type is most sensitive to blue. We see all the colors because these three receptors work in combination.

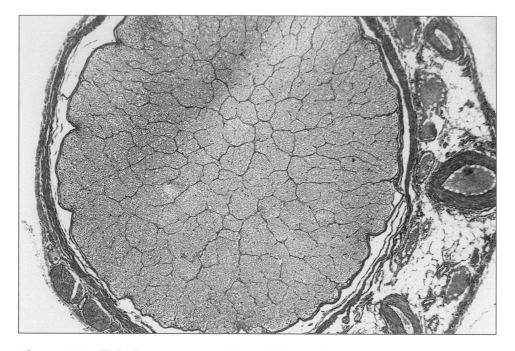

Figure 5.2 **This is a cross section of the optic nerve as seen under a high-power microscope.**

respond to the colors and shapes. This information travels through the optic nerve to the thalamus and then to a special area on the back of Mark's brain called the visual cortex (Figure 5.2). The visual cortex is located in the occipital lobe. In the visual cortex, the different colors and shapes on Mark's drawing are processed by different neurons.

The bell rang one more time, announcing the end of art class. Mark felt a knot in his stomach again: the talent show was about to begin.

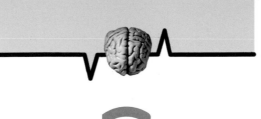

6

Controlling and Relieving Stress

The school cafeteria was bursting with activity as teachers and students prepared for the talent show. Mark walked slowly toward the group of kids that were signed up to play musical instruments. They waited backstage for their turn to perform in front of a crowd of students, teachers, and parents.

The first students on stage performed magic tricks, followed by a group of girls wearing bright-colored dresses who danced to traditional songs of far away countries. Then, two of Mark's friends, dressed in black uniforms, demonstrated their martial arts abilities, including acrobatic exercises that resulted in an ovation from the crowd.

FIGHT OR FLIGHT?

Mark's time to perform was fast approaching. Mr. Mozart, the music teacher, was pushing a piano to the stage. "This is it," Mark thought. The time had come to decide whether or not he was going to perform.

Mark felt a sinking sensation in his stomach and his palms began to sweat. Why was he feeling this way? The "fight or flight" response is a complicated body reaction that involves several parts of Mark's brain and other parts of his body. Mark's fear of performing in front of a crowd was processed by the amygdala while another part of his brain, the hypothalamus, picked up the emotion in Mark's amygdala through nerves that connect both areas.

When the hypothalamus detects fear, it sends a nerve signal to the **adrenal glands**, located on the top of Mark's kidneys. They respond by secreting the hormone **adrenaline** into the blood. Adrenaline is one of the best-known stress hormones, which quickly increases the heart rate and the breathing rate. It also increases the amount of sugar in the blood by stimulating the liver to take sugar out of storage and secrete it in the blood. This response ensures that when Mark faces the crowd, or decides to escape, his brain and muscles will have plenty of oxygen and sugar to perform (Figure 6.1).

Mr. Mozart approached Mark's group and gave the kids some useful advice. "You probably feel a little nervous about performing in front of a crowd and that's normal. To feel less nervous, take deep breaths instead of short ones. You know the composition you are about to play, so when you walk on that stage, forget about the audience and think only of the music; pretend you are playing the piece at home."

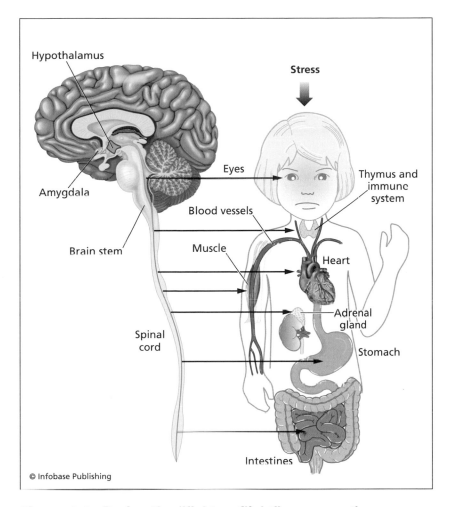

Hypothalamus

Stress

Eyes

Thymus and immune system

Amygdala

Blood vessels

Brain stem

Muscle

Heart

Adrenal gland

Spinal cord

Stomach

Intestines

© Infobase Publishing

Figure 6.1 During the "fight or flight" response the amygdala and the hypothalamus work together to stimulate many organs of the body. As a result, heart rate increases, muscles tense, sight becomes sharper, and one may feel "butterflies" in his or her stomach.

Mark took a couple of deep breaths and thought about the musical piece he was supposed to play. He knew it well—he had played it numerous times at home and with his piano teacher. After all, it was the theme from his favorite movie. Mark felt more confident now and he knew he would not forget how to play the melody. He decided he would pretend he was at home playing it for his friends.

THE PERFORMANCE

Mark sat on the piano bench, breathing calmly. Mr. Mozart announced Mark's performance and Mark placed his fingers on the keyboard. Then, for a second, his mind went blank. He could not remember how to begin. His heart raced. He knew how to play it because he had practiced it many times in the past. He had played for his piano teacher, his family, and his friends. Why had his brain forgotten it now? Stage fright is the answer. When Mark became anxious about the performance, the feeling of anxiety increased the normal **neural** firings (Figure 6.2). His neurons began firing too fast and randomly, making it hard for his brain to reach for specific memories among all the increased "firing noise" caused by his anxiety. Mark also had a hard time perceiving his environment.

Taking a few deep breaths helped Mark reduce his anxiety and he regained control of his senses as well as access to his well-established memories. "I know this!" he thought. In an instant, the hours of practice paid off. With the help of his hypothalamus, Mark remembered the exact notes and played the composition from beginning to end without further problems.

When he finished, the crowd clapped and cheered. Mark felt relief, and his heart rate and breathing slowly returned to their normal levels. His adrenal glands slowed down the

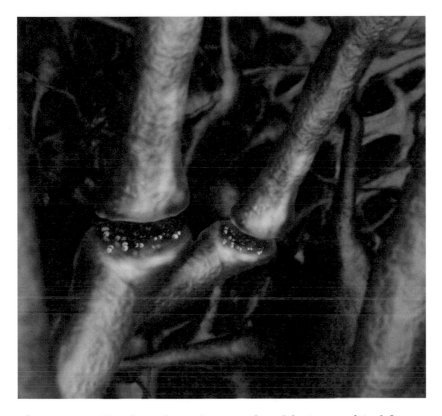

Figure 6.2 The junction where a signal is transmitted from one neuron to another is known as a synapse. Two synapses are depicted in this illustration.

production of adrenaline, until it reached normal levels again. It was over and Mark felt happy. Mr. Mozart patted him on the back, smiled, and showed him the exit. Mark could not believe that his stage performance had only lasted a few minutes. It seemed like much longer to him.

Mark felt fine, although still a little tense. This was normal too, said Mr. Mozart, and he sent Mark to his next class—gym. Mark looked forward to exercising in physical education (PE) class.

Aerobic Exercise for a Healthy Brain

Thomas Jefferson, the third President of the United (1801–1809) States, said it best: "If the body be feeble, the mind will not be strong." Today, this statement still holds true. Of all the types of physical exercise, aerobic exercise is the best for your brain. Aerobic exercise, such as running or riding a bike, increases the heart rate for a sustained period of time. This intense activity affects the brain in a positive way.

In one study, students who performed intense aerobic exercise three times a week for six weeks improved their grades when compared to students who also performed physical activities but did not increase their heart rate significantly for a sustained period. The students who performed aerobic exercises also felt less depressed and had more self-esteem.

Aerobic exercise has a similar effect in animals. Laboratory mice that run regularly are better than "couch potato" mice at learning and remembering tasks. Mice that did aerobic exercise learned how to find a way out of a maze better than the mice that did not do aerobic exercise. When the scientists studied the brains of these mice, they saw that the neurons in the hippocampus of the active mice lived longer than the neurons from mice that did not run regularly. The hippocampus is a region important for learning and memory.

The benefits of aerobic exercise take place only if the exercise is regular, not a one-time-a-week thing. As long as the mice and people pump up their hearts at least three times a week, their bodies will not be feeble and their minds will stay strong.

BEYOND STAYING FIT:
OTHER BENEFITS OF EXERCISE

Mr. Jordan, the PE teacher, announced that the class would practice basketball skills and later play a short game. They began by stretching their arms, legs, and back. Mark felt that stretching helped his muscles relax and relieved some of the tension he felt after the performance. Next, Mr. Jordan asked the students to jog four times around the basketball court.

After jogging, Mark felt his heart racing and sweat sprinkled his forehead. This reaction, however, although it looks just like a "fight or flight" response, occurs for different reasons. When Mark jogged, his muscles were working hard. To keep running, the muscles needed oxygen, sugar, and other nutrients provided by the blood. Mark's heart, which is also a muscle, beats harder to supply the increased demand for blood. His lungs work faster to provide more oxygen and eliminate the carbon dioxide produced by his body. Mark's brain senses that active muscles demand more oxygen and sugar than when they are at rest, and signals to increase the supply.

The intense work of Mark's muscles produces heat that warms up his body. Again, his brain senses the increase in body temperature and signals the skin to sweat. Sweating helps Mark cool off, just like water would cool off a heated surface. The heat on Mark's skin is used to evaporate the sweat surfacing on the skin. This removes heat from the skin, reducing its temperature. Mark also cools down by fanning his face with his hand. As his body temperature returns to normal, his brain slowly reduces the sweating.

After a session of intense exercise, Mark has not only made his muscles and lungs stronger, he has also benefited

More Than Just Music to Your Ears

To increase his creativity and his ability to come up with mathematical solutions to physics problems, Nobel Prize–winning physicist Albert Einstein played the violin. What does music have to do with math? Much more than we think, the experts tell us.

Scientists at the University of California studied two groups of three-year-old children. Half of the group attended piano or singing lessons for eight months, while the other half did not. After eight months, the scores on puzzles taken by the musical kids were 80% higher than the scores of the kids who did not take music lessons. As the school year progressed, the kids who took music lessons continued improving their mathematical abilities faster than the kids who did not play music.

Scientists think that the reason for this is that, from the brain's point of view, music is similar to math. Music consists of a series of specific notes that have to be played in a particular order for the song to sound right. Math consists of a series of specific operations (sums, subtractions, multiplications, divisions, and others) that also have to be done in a particular order to get the answer right. Music and math are organized or structured ways of thinking that use the same circuits in the brain. These circuits seem to be located over large regions of the cortex.

Learning to play a musical instrument during early childhood and regular practice help the brain to develop the neural circuits that are also used when it is solving mathematical problems or three-dimensional puzzles. Regular music practice reinforces these circuits, making it easier for the growing child not only to play the instrument but also to solve complex math and engineering problems, which use the same brain circuits.

his mind. After his PE class, Mark feels tired, relaxed, and in a good mood. He is free of the stress created by his stage performance. Most people are like Mark—they feel a sense of well-being after a session of intense exercise, like running, jogging, biking, skating, swimming, or simply playing a friendly game of soccer or basketball.

How this happens exactly is not yet clear to scientists. However, scientists know that the body produces a variety of chemicals, such as **endorphins**, in response to exercise. These chemicals are likely to be involved in making Mark feel relaxed. Also, exercise provides the brain with more glucose, its main source of energy. Glucose powers neurons to produce neurotransmitters, which are essential for brain functions.

Scientists believe that when people keep a regular exercise routine, their body and mind benefit more than if they just exercise once in a while. For Mark, the end of PE class has a double benefit. It also marks the end of the school day and it is time to go home.

7

Dealing with Pain

The school bell rang for the last time that day. Mark slid his arms through the straps on his backpack and headed toward the parking lot. He released his bike from the lock that tied it to the bike stand and pedaled home. He was looking forward to soccer practice later in the afternoon. He would not miss it for anything.

THE SCRIMMAGE

Mark put on his most comfortable T-shirt and shorts. He slid his shin guards up his legs and then he pulled long, thick socks on top of them. He tied his soccer shoes tight, secured the ball and a bottle of water inside his backpack, and jumped on his bike. He pedaled to the soccer field, just a few blocks away from his home.

When practice began, Mark and his teammates stretched, ran around the field, and practiced kicking and passing drills. Mark enjoyed all these activities, but most of all he liked the scrimmage that he and his teammates would play among themselves toward the end of practice. Mark liked the scrimmage because he played with his friends and did not have the pressure of competing against another team. There would be no more "fight or flight" feelings for the day.

So, the scrimmage began. Seven players against seven players, spread over the field. The whistle blew and the players ran, kicked the ball to the goal, and tried precise passes. They fell, got up, and kept on playing. They called for the ball, laughed, and gave "high fives" to each other. The coach was about to blow the whistle when it happened.

FEELING PAIN

Mark and his friend were fighting for the ball when Mark fell and hit his head on the ground. Instantly, he felt a sharp pain on the right side of his forehead. He sat on the grass and touched where it hurt. He felt something wet and warm that trickled down his face— he was bleeding. Mark felt a bit scared. This happens when the pain signals that come from his wound reach the amygdala. The coach ran to Mark and inspected his wound. "Ouch, it hurts!" complained Mark, pulling away from the coach. Pain perception is part of Mark's sense of touch, which also perceives temperature and tactile sensations. Pain receptors, called **nociceptors**, are distributed throughout Mark's body, inside and outside.

Nociceptors are very simple. They are formed by free nerve endings embedded on the surface of the skin (Figure 7.1). When Mark cut his skin, the injured cells released chemicals,

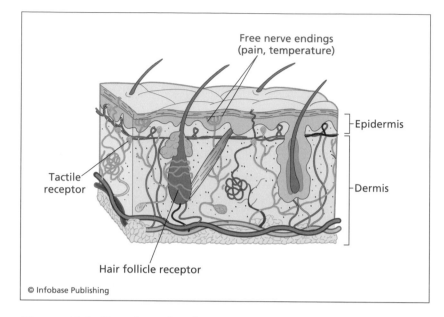

Figure 7.1 **Touch and pain receptors send signals through the spinal cord and on to the brain. Sensory receptors are found in both the epidermis (upper layer) and dermis (lower layer) of the skin.**

such as prostaglandins, that triggered a nerve impulse in the nociceptors. This message resulted in pain.

The coach pulled a clean cloth out of his first-aid kit and wiped away the blood on Mark's head. Mark tried not to complain and keep a straight face in front of his teammates, but it was hard. Every time the coach touched his forehead even slightly, Mark winced in pain because his pain receptors were constantly firing messages to the brain. They transmitted nerve impulses into the brain stem through cranial nerves. Then, the signal moved into the thalamus. From here, the nerve impulse continued its route to the sensory cortex, and Mark felt pain.

Pain messages cross over a midpoint in the brain. As a result, pain Mark feels on the right side of his forehead is processed on the left side of his brain. If Mark had hurt the left side of his forehead, then his right hemisphere would be in charge of processing the pain sensation.

Nobody likes to be in pain. It is one of the most unpleasant sensations and you may ask, "Do I need to be able to feel pain?" What would happen if you were not able to feel it? Some people are born without the ability to feel pain. Pain-free individuals often suffer from severe burns and cuts because they have no pain to warn them of danger. In extreme cases, people have died because they did not feel pain to warn them of serious infections. Sometimes, their appendix ruptured and they did not feel any pain to signal the deadly

Just Rub It

When you hit your elbow on the corner of your desk, you probably rub it to make it feel better. How does rubbing an injured elbow help reduce the pain instead of making it worse?

One explanation is that rubbing helps reduce pain sensations because the brain cannot pay attention to pain and rubbing signals at the same time. When you rub the injured elbow, you are sending a second signal for the brain to notice. The brain now divides its attention between the pain and the rubbing signals, perceiving the pain in the elbow with less intensity. Scientists call this phenomenon competitive inhibition. Another explanation suggests that rubbing sends a non-painful signal that blocks or closes the path of the pain signal. Scientists call this phenomenon pain control theory.

situation. Pain may not be pleasant, but it warns us that a part of our body is injured. Pain also helps us heal by reminding us to be careful in how we treat an injury. Ignoring pain is not a good idea, because pain might save your life.

BLOCKING PAIN

The coach continued cleaning Mark's wound until he could see how bad it was. Mark had a deep cut about an inch long. It kept bleeding, so the coach pressed on it with a clean cloth to control the loss of blood. "You need stitches," the coach said, "to close the wound and help it heal."

Mark's mother took him to the emergency room. The cut was no longer bleeding, but Dr. Livingstone confirmed the coach's prediction—it needed stitches. "The stitches hurt too," the doctor said, "so I will give you an **anesthetic**. I will inject it around the wound and it will numb the pain. Then, you won't feel a thing."

Mark felt the needle sting on the skin around his cut. Shortly after, he did not feel pain anymore. Dr. Livingstone gave Mark seven stitches that did not hurt at all. Mark could touch the skin around the wound without hurting. The pain killer had lived up to its name.

Pain relievers work in different ways. The anesthesia the doctor injected into Mark's skin worked by blocking the nociceptors that transmit the pain sensation to the brain. Some types of anesthesia block the neurotransmitters that pass on the nerve impulse from one neuron to the next, after the nociceptors sent the signal. This stops the signal from reaching the brain. Other pain relievers, such as aspirin and ibuprofen, work by stopping the injured cells from releasing the chemicals that trigger the nerve impulse in the nociceptors (Figure

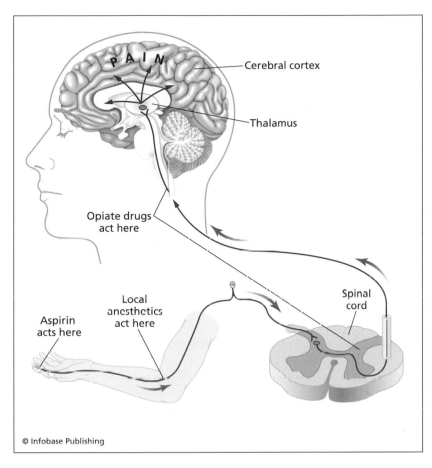

Figure 7.2 Different pain killers act on different areas of the nervous system. Aspirin acts by reducing pain signals in the distant peripheral nerves, such as those in the finger. Local anesthetics block pain signals traveling up the nerve, while opiate drugs act mostly in the central nervous system.

7.2). Dr. Livingstone prescribed a pain reliever that would work this way to stop the pain while Mark's injury healed.

The doctor finished stitching Mark's wound and sent him home. Mark could not wait to go to sleep.

A Monument to a Gas

It is hard to imagine having surgery or an operation without anesthesia or a pain killer. But it happened many times in the past before doctors figured out a way to stop people from feeling pain. Before 1846, doctors in the United States operated on people without giving them something to stop the pain. This brought much suffering during and after the operation.

It is not a surprise, then, that there is a monument in honor of the first time doctors used an anesthetic. The discovery that the gas ether is capable of causing people to pass out and not feel pain was immediately applied to surgery. People inhaled the gas, closed their eyes, and looked like they were asleep. But they were more than asleep—they would not wake up if you shook them or called them aloud. They would not wake up even if a doctor operated on them. They would wake up by themselves after the ether had been removed by their bodies. Ether was the first anesthetic used to prevent pain during surgery and it deserved a monument for saving people from tremendous suffering.

The monument to ether stands in the Boston Public Gardens, the oldest botanical garden in the United States. The monument has a statue of a man, a "Good Samaritan," giving ether to a patient. The inscription reads, "There shall be no more pain."

Doctors do not use ether anymore as anesthesia for various reasons. For example, it was hard to know the right amount of ether a person should breathe to remain unconscious. Also, ether is highly flammable. Since the discovery of ether, scientists have found many more chemicals—gases and liquids—that are also anesthetics and work better than ether.

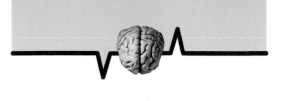

8

A Good Night's Sleep

The only thing Mark wanted to do when he got home was to go to bed. What had started as a regular day ended up bringing two unexpected events to Mark's routine. First, he had forgotten about his piano performance in the school's talent show. Then, he got hurt during soccer practice. At the end of the day, his head hurt, his leg muscles felt sore from soccer practice, and he was very tired. A good night's sleep, Dr. Livingstone said, would make him feel better tomorrow.

As soon as Mark got home, he changed his clothes and ate dinner. He watched TV in bed for 30 minutes before falling asleep. When Mark sleeps, his brain is active even though it does not seem to be. During sleep, Mark does not move much, his eyes are closed, and he does not seem to be aware of his surroundings. Nevertheless, his brain is up and running. It remains active, but its pattern or type of activity is different from the pattern it has when Mark is awake.

THE SLEEPING BRAIN

Mark spends one-third of his life sleeping. All other mammals, birds, fish, and reptiles sleep too. This is good evidence that sleeping is a fundamental activity for animals, even if it seems that nothing is going on during sleep. However, if we could look inside Mark's brain while he's sleeping, we would see that his brain is not inactive.

When Mark rested his head on the pillow and closed his eyes, his brain and body began to change their activities. Mark's body relaxed and his heart rate and breathing slowed down. His senses did not perceive external sensations and his body barely moved. During the eight to ten hours that Mark sleeps every night, his brain will show two types or patterns of activity. Scientists call these brain activities SWS (slow wave sleep) and REM (rapid eye movement).

Scientists detect these patterns when they measure the electrical activity of Mark's brain during sleep using a machine called an **electroencephalograph (EEG)**. To measure the brain's electrical activity, a doctor places special sensors called electrodes that record small amounts of electricity on the patient's skull. The electrodes are connected to a machine that records or draws a picture of the electric waves produced by the brain (Figure 8.1). SWS and REM show very different brain wave patterns in an EEG. These wave patterns are also different from the electrical activity produced by Mark's brain when he is awake.

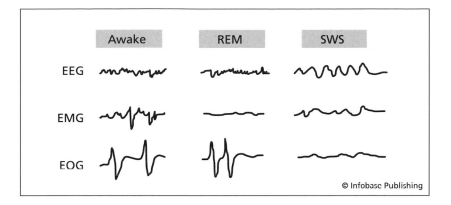

Figure 8.1 An EEG (electroencephalogram) is a measure of brain activity, an EMG (electromyogram) shows muscle activity, while an EOG (electroculogram) measures eye movements. In this illustration, the three are compared while a subject is awake and in two different stages of sleep.

In addition to measuring the electrical activity of the brain, scientists use other machines to measure how the muscles of the eyes move during sleep. The records of these three body activities— brain wave patterns, muscle movements, and eye movements—clearly show that both the body and the brain are always active, some times more than others, during sleep and waking times. Throughout the night, Mark's brain cycles between SWS and REM sleep.

When Mark was awake, his brain showed rapid, short waves of electrical activity. But as soon as he closed his eyes, the brain waves slowly began to change to a slow wave pattern. Mark's brain waves now look larger (an increase in amplitude) and slower (reduction in the frequency). During this period of SWS, Mark's muscles may move, for example, when he unknowingly changes his body position.

Looking at the Brain Work: Imaging Techniques

When scientists first studied the brain hundreds of years ago, they could only look at brains of dead people or animals. It was impossible to look at the working brain of a living person. Today, this has changed: scientists now have imaging technologies to see the living brain in action.

Imaging techniques allow scientists and doctors to see an image of the brain without even touching the skull of the individual. The images show which parts of the brain are active and which are inactive when a person performs a specific task. Imaging also has helped scientists understand how drugs affect the brain. These methods can also show how an injured or diseased brain functions differently from a healthy brain.

◆ **Positron Emission Tomography (PET)**—This imaging technique measures how the brain works by showing changes in blood flow when a specific brain area is active. If, for example, a person is performing a visual task, such as following a dot on a computer screen, then the brain area within the occipital lobe (the visual cortex) will show an increase in blood flow.

◆ **Magnetic Resonance Imaging (MRI)**—MRI scans allow scientists to take three-dimensional pictures of the brain (or any other organ). These images help scientists understand how the structure of the brain changes when the brain is damaged or diseased (Figure 8.2). For an MRI scan, a person lies inside a massive, hollow cylindrical magnet that looks like a tunnel and is exposed to a powerful magnetic field. The patient does not feel the magnetic field and is not harmed. Pulses of magnetic waves affect the hydrogen molecules in the body, and the machine detects radio signals produced by the hydrogen atoms. With the help of a computer, it turns the signals into a three-dimensional image of the brain.

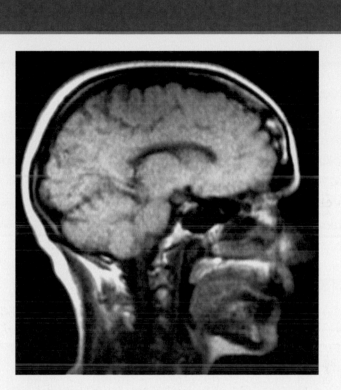

Figure 8.2 Scientists use magnetic resonance imaging (MRI) to examine areas of the brain that may be diseased or injured.

◆ **Functional Magnetic Resonance Imaging (fMRI)—While an MRI provides still, three-dimensional images of the brain, an fMRI adds a measurement of brain activity. Therefore, doctors and scientists can see a three-dimensional picture of the brain while it is performing certain activities. An fMRI does this by measuring changes in the oxygen levels in the blood, which vary according to the activity that neurons are performing. Functional MRI allows scientists to map the brain and see the activity in different areas.**

After a short time in SWS, Mark's brain will switch its activity to REM. His body does not move during this period, except for his eyes. Scientists discovered REM sleep when they observed that although the eyes are closed, people's eyeballs move in all directions rapidly. This is very easy to see, so scientists named this period rapid eye movement (REM) sleep.

During REM sleep, Mark's brain changes its slow and wide wave pattern to a rapid and small wave pattern. This resembles the wave pattern his brain has when he is awake. However, Mark is far from being awake; the rest of his body, except for his eyes, is fully relaxed and still. It is during REM sleep that Mark is most likely to dream.

MYSTERIOUS DREAMS

Mark dreams most often during REM sleep. If his alarm clock wakes him when he is in REM sleep, he will probably remember his dream. But his memory of it would soon fade. If Mark wishes to remember a dream, he writes it down as soon as he wakes up.

In his dreams, Mark may be doing ordinary things with people he knows, like playing soccer with his friends. But sometimes Mark dreams that he is doing things he could not possibly do when he was awake, such as flying like a bird or breathing underwater like a fish. Sometimes, Mark may have nightmares that suddenly wake him up.

Why people dream is still an unsolved mystery. However, scientists know that people need REM sleep. If for some reason one night Mark woke up every time his brain entered REM sleep, then the next night he would spend most of his sleeping hours in REM sleep instead of alternating between SWS and REM sleep cycles. It would be as if his brain needed to catch up with all the REM sleep it missed the night before.

Sleepless Babies

Human babies may sleep as much as 16 hours a day, while children and adults usually rest for 6 to 10 hours. You have probably seen that newborn puppies sleep a great deal too, while older puppies and adult dogs spend less time sleeping and more time being active. For many years, scientists believed that newborn babies of all animal species required lots of sleep to allow their brains and body to grow and develop, but in June 2005, scientists discovered that this was not always the case. The scientists were surprised when they found the first exception to this apparent rule for babies. Baby dolphins and baby orcas (killer whales) do not sleep during the first month after birth. Instead, they swim or move constantly, keeping both eyes open all the time. Their mothers do not sleep either.

After three to four weeks, the baby dolphins and orcas begin to sleep. Their mothers also begin to sleep again. Being able to live without sleep for one month is unheard of for any other animal. Scientists think that the reason baby dolphins and baby orcas do not go to sleep during the first four weeks after birth is to stay on the move to avoid predators. They also need to keep moving to keep their bodies warm while they grow a thick layer of blubber to help them survive in cold water.

WHY MARK SLEEPS

When Mark sleeps every night, his brain remains active, but in a different way than when he is awake. Does Mark really need sleep or could he have a normal life without it?

If Mark did not get enough sleep for a few consecutive days because he was sick, for example, he would have trouble doing the usual things he does at school. His memory, attention, and performance in sports would diminish significantly. Without enough sleep, Mark would have trouble remembering the material he studied in preparation for a test. He would make more mistakes when doing his homework because his attention would falter. His reflexes would be slower, turning him into a poor soccer player. He would have little energy to move around, and he would be tired all the time. As Dr. Livingstone said, he just needs a good night sleep.

What happens exactly in Mark's brain and body when he sleeps is not completely understood. But we do know that if he did not sleep at all for a few days, he would eventually feel very anxious and exhausted. Sleep is essential for Mark's brain and body to stay healthy and fully active. If Mark wants to keep his body strong and his mind sharp, he cannot skip sleep. In fact, he cannot live without it.

Many scientists think that while we sleep, our brains are busy consolidating or securing memories of things we learned during our waking hours. If Mark had memorized a new set of states and capitals of the United States in class, he would remember them better after a good night's sleep. But he would remember them poorly if he woke up many times during his sleep. A good night's sleep helps his brain turn new information into a long-term memory that would be harder to forget.

A good night's sleep is also necessary to replenish Mark's body stamina or energy. He would feel weak and tired after a short or an interrupted sleep time. During sleep, his body replenishes any lost energy and he will feel rested in the morning. Sleep is essential for Mark to be able to learn in school, to do his best at soccer practice, and to deal with unexpected situations. Sleep is not a waste of time for Mark's body. It is an activity necessary for a healthy, productive, and enjoyable life.

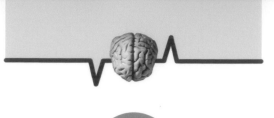

Myths and Truths About the Brain

The more scientists study the brain, the better they can separate the myths from the truths about this mysterious and fascinating organ. Here are seven of the myths and truths about the human brain.

WE ONLY USE 10% OF OUR BRAIN (MYTH)

You have probably heard the saying: "You use only 10% of your brain." Is this true? Do we only use a very small portion of our brain?

Today, neuroscientists dismiss this idea, and they have evidence to prove it is a myth. Scientists do not know for certain when this idea began or what observations prompted it, but evidence shows

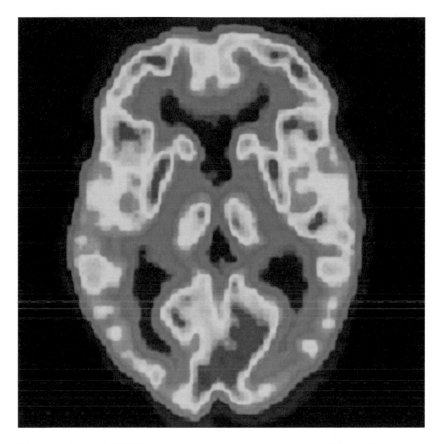

Figure 9.1 **A PET scan measures changes in blood flow when a specific brain area is active.**

that all parts of the brain function, not just 10%. One of the strongest pieces of evidence comes from imaging the active brain. When scientists scan the brain using positron emission tomography, or PET (Figure 9.1), they see that much of the brain is active when it is performing many different tasks. The scans also show that during particular tasks, some areas are more active than others.

For example, Dr. Livingstone did a PET scan on Mark's brain while Mark looked at a dot's movement in a maze. The PET scan revealed high activity in the visual cortex in the occipital area of Mark's brain, which is, the place that deals with visual tasks. At the same time, other areas in Mark's brain also showed activity. This activity represents other tasks that Mark's brain is doing at the same time, such as using the computer keyboard to record his observations for the visual test. In this case, the brain area in charge of controlling Mark's movements, the motor cortex, shows activity.

The statement that we use only 10% or our brain is a myth. We use all of our brain as we go through the different mental and physical activities we perform every day, including sleep.

THE HUMAN BRAIN COMPENSATES FOR MISSING SENSORS (*TRUTH*)

You may have heard that people who have lost one sense learn to make up for it by improving the use of the other senses. For example, people say that blind individuals hear better than sighted people. Is it true that after losing a sense the brain tries to compensate?

Scientists agree that the loss of one sense prompts the brain to use the other senses better. However, scientists still disagree on how this happens. Some scientists think that blind people develop a more sensitive sense of hearing than sighted people. They say that some time after they lost their sight, blind people would be able to hear sounds that sighted people are not able to hear. Other scientists say that blind and sighted people are able to detect the same sounds, but blind people have learned to pay better attention to those sounds that are the hardest to hear. Either way, it is true that after losing a sense the brain will make better use of the other senses.

THE BRAIN WORKS ON THE PRINCIPLE OF "USE IT OR LOSE IT" (*TRUTH*)

Mark broke his left leg one day when he fell while riding his bike. Dr. Livingstone put a cast on the leg. For six weeks, Mark's leg muscles did not move. When the doctor removed the cast, Mark was surprised to see how small his left leg muscles were compared to his right leg muscles. When Mark asked Dr. Livingstone why this had happened, he explained that muscles get smaller when they are not used for a long period of time. "It happens to all muscles," Dr. Livingstone said. "Use it or lose it. Muscles need exercise to stay strong."

The same rule applies to the brain. If the brain does not "exercise" or receive the necessary input from the environment to develop a particular ability, then that ability will be lost.

Let's see what happened in Mark's brain when he began learning to play the piano. After taking his first piano lesson, Mark practiced every other day. Practice was necessary to teach his brain the correct position and movements of the fingers. Repetition is the key to train the brain in any task, both physical and mental. Every time Mark repeated the same hand movements on the keyboard, the same circuit of neurons fired together in his brain. The more times the same neurons fire together, the stronger their physical connection will be. If Mark just repeated the piano exercises once or twice a week, the circuit of neurons would have lost their

Not Always Famous

Today, we know that the brain is very important because it is the place where thinking and feeling takes place. The brain allows us to perceive the environment and interact with it; it regulates what our body does. But people did not always think so highly of the brain.

More than 3,000 years ago, the ancient Egyptians wrote the oldest known books about the brain and other organs in the body. In the time of the Pharaohs, people thought that the heart was the most important organ in the body. They thought that thinking and feeling took place in the heart, not the brain.

The Egyptians demonstrated this belief when they mummified their Pharaohs and other important people. The first step in mummification was to scoop out the brain through the nostrils with an iron hook. The brain was discarded but the heart and other internal organs were preserved so that they could be used again in the afterlife.

It was not only the ancient Egyptians who shared this belief. Ancient civilizations in Mesopotamia, India, and China placed the heart first and did not consider the brain as important. They did not give the brain its due importance until much later in history.

The brain moved up in importance by the middle of the fifth century B.C. It was Alcmaeon, a Greek from the city of Croton, who promoted the brain to its rightful place as the center of sensation, thought, and feeling as we know it today. Alcmaeon studied the sense of vision. He was among the first to describe that individual nerves leave each eye and come together "behind the forehead" (this is the correct location of the occipital cortex, where vision is processed). He suggested that the nerves were paths to the brain, and he was right. Although the nerves do not carry light, they carry electric signals to the brain that allow us to see.

connection. If he did not "use it" long enough, he would "lose" the link between the neurons involved in playing the piano.

Mark knows that to restore the strength in his left leg muscles, he just has to exercise them regularly. In a similar way, Mark can keep his mind sharp throughout his life with physical exercise, by learning new things, and by regularly practicing what he learns. If he does not want to lose it, he must use it.

BRAIN DAMAGE IS *ALWAYS* FOREVER (*MYTH*)

It is a very good idea to follow the advice Dr. Livingstone gave to Mark when he was stitching the cut on Mark's head. "I can help your body repair this cut. But try not to damage your brain because there are injuries we still cannot fix." It is true that brain damage is something everybody should try to avoid because the consequences can be permanent, but this is not always the case.

For many years, scientists believed that the brain lacked the ability to fix itself. Scientists thought that once you lost neurons, the function they coordinated, such as speech or movement, would be permanently affected. This idea has changed. Scientists have discovered that sometimes the brain is capable of recovering lost functions. Some patients who had lost their ability to move their right arm after damage to the left hemisphere of the brain did recover the use of their arm, at least part of it, after physical therapy or exercise. Doctors studied the patients' brains and discovered that their brains had changed. Therapy and exercise stimulated the brain to use healthy neurons around the site of injury to rewire the lost connections between the arm and the brain.

Neighboring neurons took on the job of the dead neurons and restored the ability to move the arm.

Today, we know that the brain has the ability to rewire its neural connections. It does it in response to external stimuli, both physical (such as playing the piano) and mental (such as learning multiplication factors). However, when the damage to the brain is too severe, rewiring might not be enough to recover the lost function.

BRAIN CELLS CANNOT MULTIPLY AND MAKE NEW CELLS (*MYTH*)

Until the 1990s, scientist thought that neurons could not divide or reproduce to make new neurons that would replace old, damaged, or dead neurons. They thought that other cells in the body were able to reproduce, but not neurons. That meant that once a neuron died, it would never be replaced with a new cell. If a large number of neurons died, then unless the brain rewired the lost function with other neurons already available, the function would be lost permanently.

Fortunately, scientists were wrong—there are neurons in the brain that can reproduce. Scientists have found them in two places inside the brain: near the **ventricles** and inside the hippocampus. The ventricles are spaces or cavities in the brain filled with **cerebrospinal fluid**, and the hippocampus is a brain area that is essential for learning and memory.

This very important discovery has changed the way scientists think about the brain. The brain is no longer viewed as an unchanging organ, but one that is flexible and capable of changing itself. This discovery has also brought hope to people with severe brain damage and to those affected by

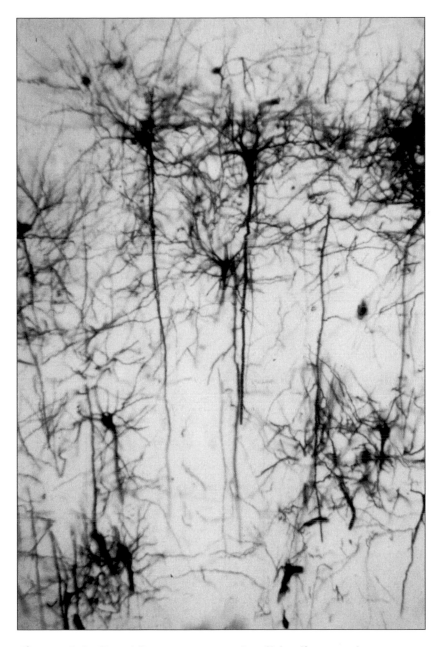

Figure 9.2 Dendrites, axons, and cell bodies can be seen in this photograph of neurons of the cerebral cortex.

brain disorders. Scientists have also succeeded at growing new neurons in the laboratory (Figure 9.2). One day, doctors might be able to fix brain injuries and cure diseases by replacing damaged or sick cells with new neurons that would restore the brain to its normal function.

THE HUMAN BRAIN WORKS LIKE A COMPUTER (*MYTH/TRUTH*)

Is your brain like a computer? Does it work like one? Brains and computers have a lot in common, but they are also different in many ways. Here is how brains and computers are similar and different.

Similarity #1: Brains and computers both need energy to work.

Difference #1: Computers use electrical energy that comes from an electric plug in your house. Brains, on the other hand, get their energy from the sugar glucose that comes from the food you eat and the oxygen you breathe.

Similarity #2: Brains and computers use electrical signals to transmit information.

Difference #2: Computers transmit electrical signals through cables made of wires, while brain signals travel through nerves formed by living neurons. Electric messages travel faster in computers, almost at the speed of light or about 187,500 miles per second (300,000 km/second). Electric messages travel much slower in nerves: the fastest nerves transmit messages at approximately 260 miles per hour (about 420 km/hour). Also, in computers, electric messages can be turned "on" or "off," while the brain is never off. Even when you are sleeping, the brain shows electrical activity.

Similarity #3: Brains and computers are able to perceive changes in their environment and act upon them. Many complex machines have computers built inside them that improve the machine's performance. Some cars, for example, have computers with sensors that detect the direction the vehicle is going and compare it to the direction the driver is trying to steer it. If the computer detects that the car is not going where the driver wants it to go, it will take action to bring the car's movement back in line with the driver's intentions.

So, if the road is wet and the rear wheels of the car lose traction and slip when the driver is making a turn, the driver could lose the ability to turn the car along the curve and slide off the road. That is when the computer helps the driver regain control of the car by sending a signal immediately to apply the outside front wheel brake and prevent loss of control.

In a similar way, the brain knows if we lose balance when we walk and sends the necessary signals to our muscles to avoid falling and getting hurt. If Mark is running on a muddy field and his left foot slips, his brain will perceive the loss of balance and will send the signals to change his body motion, such as stepping firmly with the right foot or putting his hands in front to prevent falling and regain his balanced position.

Difference #3: Brains are different from computers in that brains also respond to external stimuli with emotions, while computers do not. If Mark was about to fall but managed to regain his balance, he might feel a bit nervous or scared afterwards because he knows that he might have hurt himself. The car computer, on the other hand, simply went back to monitoring the car's movements through its sensors. It did not feel a thing for having been able to prevent an accident.

Similarity #4: Both brains and computers can store memories.

Difference #4: Computers store memories in specific electronic devices in the computer, such as disks, chips, and CD-ROMs. Brains store memories not in one place, but in many neuronal circuits in the brain.

Similarity #5: Brains and computers can be damaged.

Computers and brains are protected by a hard and sturdy case. A bone-hard skull protects the brain, and metal and plastic cases protect delicate computer parts. In spite of this protection, both brains and computers may get damaged. Computers may get a "virus" or a "worm" that makes them malfunction. A computer may get wet, overheat, or the user may drop it, causing the computer to stop working properly. The brain may also get sick with bacteria or a virus, or neurons may stop producing neurotransmitters. The brain may begin to bleed and swell if a person hits his or her head hard enough.

Difference #5: If a computer fails, it can be fixed or its broken parts replaced. In the worst case, you could buy a new one. Brains cannot be fixed so easily. There are no replacement parts. However, scientists are working hard to find ways to repair damaged brains, and there is hope for cures in the future.

Brains and computers are different in two other important ways. First, brains are capable of imagination, but not computers. Thanks to your brain, you can come up with new ways to solve problems or create an exciting story, a moving musical composition, or an inspiring work of art. Computers, so far, have not written any original books or created a work of art capable of triggering emotions in people.

Second, and this may be the most important difference between brains and computers, is consciousness. Thanks to the brain, people are conscious, meaning they are aware they exist, who they are, and where they are. Computers are not aware of their existence, at least for now. But scientists continue improving computers and one day in the future it might be possible for these amazing machines to have imagination and become aware of their existence, just like many science fiction movies predict.

THE BRAIN IS "HARD-WIRED" FROM THE TIME WE ARE BORN (*MYTH*)

Old books written about the brain described it as an essential organ that was "hard-wired" from the time of birth. This meant that the way the billions of neurons were connected to each other, the circuits they formed by the time we were born, would not change throughout life. They stated that this "immutable or unchangeable wiring" was essential for the brain to perform all its functions. Neural circuits needed to stay fixed so we could coordinate body movements, perceive the environment through our senses, and store memories. If the wiring changed, how could we remember anything? How could we keep being who we are throughout life?

This static or fixed view of the brain has changed radically. Today, we see the brain not as an unchanging organ but as one that is capable of changing its shape by rewiring the billions of connections that form it.

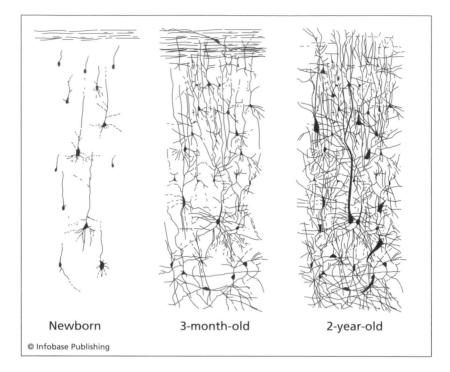

Newborn   3-month-old   2-year-old

© Infobase Publishing

Figure 9.3 **The number of connections among the neurons in the cerebral cortex increases dramatically from birth to two years of age.**

When a baby is born, there are few neurons in the cortex, but after three months the number of dendrites or cell projections emerging from the bodies and axons of neurons has multiplied enormously. The processes of sprouting dendrites and establishing synapses (cell-to-cell connections) grow at a tremendous pace. The result is that when the baby is two years old, the cortex is much thicker than just after birth and the neural connections or circuits are massively more complex (Figure 9.3).

This type of huge growth and immense wiring occurs mostly in the first years after birth. However, it never stops.

As we grow up and enter adulthood, the process continues at a much slower pace. When Mark learns new skills, such as bouncing a soccer ball many times on his head without dropping it, or memorizing all the states and capitals of the United States, his brain changes. After much practice, his brain establishes the wiring necessary to commit the skill or knowledge to memory. The more times he repeats the states and capitals, the stronger the wiring will be and the better and longer he will remember them.

Learning new things and improving what you already know with regular practice gives your brain a good workout. People who work out their brains turn them into organs that are healthier and stronger than couch-potato brains. What would you rather have—an exercised brain or a couch-potato brain?

10

Activities
to Exercise
Your Brain

Inside your head is one of the most important organs of your body—the brain. Just like Mark, you need your brain every day, all the time. You depend on it to do everything you want to do. There is no doubt that you want to take good care of your brain and learn as much as you can about it. In this chapter, the first two experiments will help you take care of your brain. Taking care of your brain is about protecting it and exercising it to keep it "in shape." You will test the value of helmets in the first experiment, and you will exercise your short-term memory in the second experiment. The more you exercise your memory, the better it will get. The rest of the experiments will allow you to better understand your brain and how it works. You will learn a number of neat facts about your brain, such as how you can trick your sense of taste. So, read on and have fun exercising your brain!

DESIGN THE BEST EGG HELMET

When you get ready to go running, you never forget to wear your running shoes. You know that if you do not, you will probably injure your feet. An easy way to avoid foot injuries is to wear the proper shoes. So, when you ride your bike or skateboard, do you always wear a helmet?

Even if you are an experienced rider, there is always a chance you could fall from a bike or skateboard. And head injuries can be very serious. Experts have confirmed that wearing a helmet reduces the risk of head injury by 85%. It is easy to get the odds in your favor and reduce your chances of head injury—just wear your helmet. And pass the word around to your friends: do not go biking, skating, or roller-blading without wearing a helmet.

You may ask, "Does a helmet really protect the head from injury?" Try this experiment to check it out. In this experiment, you will use raw eggs to represent your head. The shell is the skull and the egg inside is your brain. Use different materials to make a helmet for your eggs and see if they protect them from injury.

Materials

- Eggs, raw (4–6)
- Small styrofoam cups
- Egg carton
- Foam
- Paper
- Tape
- Other materials you would like to try

◆ Newspaper (to cover your testing area and clean it easily afterward)
◆ Markers to decorate your egg (optional)

Procedure

1 Cut and shape your materials, Styrofoam cups, egg carton, paper, and foam, to fit on the eggs like helmets. Secure the helmets with tape.
2 Set up your test area: cover an area on a hard floor with 2–3 pieces of newspaper.
3 Drop an unprotected egg on the newspaper-covered surface from about 12 inches above the floor. Did it break?
4 Drop the eggs wearing the helmets. Did they break?
5 Are helmets useful to protect eggs (and heads) from cracking?

● ● ● ● ●

WHAT'S MISSING?

Test your friends' short-term memory by determining if they remember what's missing in this experiment.

Materials

◆ Large tray with 10 different small objects on it (for example, a nickel, a pen, a marble, an eraser, a stone, etc.)
◆ A large cloth to cover the tray completely
◆ Paper and pencil for your friends to write what they remember

Procedure

1 Have your friends sit at a table and place the covered tray with the objects in front of them.

2 Explain to your friends that you will uncover the tray for one minute, and you want them to look at the objects and remember as many as they can. Uncover the tray.

3 After one minute, cover the tray. Ask your friends to write down the objects they remember. How many of your friends remember all the objects? How many remember fewer than five?

4 Without your friends looking, remove four objects from the tray and cover it again.

5 Uncover the tray for one minute and ask your friends to determine which objects are missing and write them down. How many remember all the missing objects? How many remember at least one?

• • • • •

LEFT SIDE OR RIGHT SIDE?

About 90% of the population is right-handed, meaning that they prefer to use their right hand for most tasks. But do they also prefer to use their right ear, eye, and foot? Try this experiment with your friends and find out, but do not tell them what the experiments are about until the end.

Right-handed or left-handed?

First, test to find out if your friend is right-handed or left-handed.

Materials

◆ Pen or pencil
◆ Paper
◆ Scissors
◆ Ball
◆ Cup with water

Procedure

1 Sit with your friend at a table and place a pen or pencil and a piece of paper in front of him or her.
2 Ask him or her to write their name on the paper.
3 Record which hand your friend used to pick up the pencil or pen to write with.
4 Place the scissors in front of your friend and ask him or her to pick it up and cut a square out of the piece of paper.
5 Record which hand was used to pick up the scissor and cut the paper.
6 Both of you stand up. Give him or her the ball and ask your friend to throw it to you.
7 Record which hand was used to get and throw the ball.
8 Grab the ball and ask your friend to use just one hand to catch it.
9 Throw the ball and record which hand he or she used to catch it.
10 Sit back at the table and offer your friend a drink of water. Which hand did he or she use to drink? Record the result.

Right ear or left ear?

Find out which is your friend's favored ear.

Materials

- ◆ Small box with a small object inside (marble or pencil)
- ◆ Phone

Procedure

1 Stand behind your friend. Tell him or her that you are going to whisper and that you want your friend to listen very closely.
2 Speak very quietly and see which ear your friend uses to hear your whisper. Record the result.
3 Give your friend the box containing an object. Ask him or her to shake the box and try to identify what is inside the box by putting an ear close to the box. Record which ear he or she uses to listen to the box.
4 Place the phone on the table and ask your friend to pretend it is ringing and to answer the call. To which ear did he or she lift the phone? Record the result.

Right eye or left eye?

Find out which is your friend's favored eye.

Materials

- ◆ Paper or cardboard tube
- ◆ Paper with a small hole in the middle (about the size of a dime)

Procedure

1 Give the paper or cardboard tube to your friend and ask him or her to look through it. Which eye does your friend put to the tube? Record the result.
2 Give your friend the paper with the small hole in the middle. Ask him or her to extend their arms forward and use both eyes and look at a distant object, like a decoration hanging on a wall, through the hole.
3 Now, ask your friend to bring the paper closer and closer to his or her face while still looking at the object on the wall. Which eye does the paper finally reach? Record your result.

Left or right foot?

Which is your friend's favored foot?

Materials

◆ Ball
◆ Stairs
◆ Paper ball

Procedure

1 Place the ball on the floor and ask your friend to kick it with his or her foot. Which foot was used? Record the result.
2 Ask your friend to stand in front of the stairs. Ask him or her to step up onto the first step. Which foot did he or she lift? Record your result.

3 Place a paper ball on the floor in front of your friend's feet. Ask him or her to stomp on the paper ball. Which foot was used? Record your result.

Look at the results and tell your friend which are his or her favored hand, ear, eye, and foot. If your friend is right-handed, does he or she also prefer the right ear, eye, and foot?

• • • • •

TRICKING YOUR SENSE OF TASTE

Do sweet things always taste sweet and bitter things always taste bitter? It all depends on what your taste buds tasted before. Try the toothpaste test.

Materials
- A glass of sweet lemonade
- A glass of drinking water
- Toothpaste containing sodium lauryl sulfate (most toothpastes do, check the list of inactive ingredients)
- New toothbrush

Procedure
1 Take a sip of lemonade. Taste the sweet flavor and also notice its bitter taste.
2 Rinse your mouth with water.
3 Brush your teeth using the toothpaste containing the detergent sodium lauryl sulfate.

4 Have another sip of lemonade. Does it taste the same as the first time? If not, how does it taste now? What happened to your taste buds?

Explanation of the results: Sodium lauryl sulfate suppresses the "sweet" sensors in the tongue and enhances the "bitter" sensors. That is why after brushing with the toothpaste, the lemonade tastes much more bitter than sweet, but just temporarily. The sweet sensors recover their sensitivity after a few minutes.

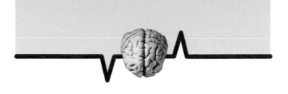

Glossary

Adrenal glands Two small organs, each located above a kidney, that secrete a variety of chemicals and hormones, including adrenaline.

Adrenaline Hormone released into the blood in response to stress that increases the heart rate and the amount of sugar in the blood; also called epinephrine.

Ambidextrous Individuals that can use their right and left hands equally.

Amygdala Brain structure involved in regulating emotions like fear and anger.

Anesthetic Drug or chemical that produces loss of sensation, pain, or consciousness.

Anosmia Loss of the sense of smell.

Astrocytes Glial cells that nourish neurons.

Auditory cortex Region of the brain involved in hearing.

Axon Long extension from the cell body of a neuron by which the cell sends information to other neurons, muscles, or glands.

Brain The most complex organ in the body, encased by the skull and formed by the cerebrum, brain stem, and cerebellum.

Brain lobes The four sections into which the cerebral cortex is divided: parietal, frontal, occipital, and temporal.

Brain stem The major area by which the brain sends information to and receives information from the spinal cord. It controls important functions like breathing and heart beat.

Broca's area Brain region located in the left hemisphere (for most people) important for the production of speech.

Caffeine A bitter chemical found in coffee, tea, and chocolate that stimulates brain activity.

Cell body Portion of a neuron that contains the nucleus.

Central nervous system (CNS) The brain and spinal cord.

Cerebellum Brain structure involved in coordinating voluntary movements, posture, and balance.

Cerebral cortex The top layer of the brain formed by gray matter involved in perception, emotion, thought, and planning.

Cerebrospinal fluid A liquid found in cavities within the brain called ventricles, and in the central canal of the spinal cord.

Cerebrum The largest part of the brain formed by two sides or hemispheres. The outer part of the cerebrum is the cerebral cortex.

Corpus callosum Large bundle of nerve fibers linking the left and right cerebral hemispheres.

Dendrite A tree-like extension of the neuron cell body that receives information from other neurons.

Electroencephalogram (EEG) A graphic record of the electrical activity of the brain.

Endorphins Pain-reducing body chemicals produced by endurance exercise.

Executive functions Advanced brain functions, such as planning, that take place in the frontal cortex.

Frontal cortex Area located at the front of the brain dedicated to high levels of thinking and movement.

Glial cells Specialized cells that nourish and support neurons.

Gustatory cortex Region of the brain involved in taste.

Gyri Curved bumps on the surface of the cerebral cortex.

Hemispheres The right and left halves of the cerebrum.

Hippocampus Area of the brain involved in memory processes.

Hypothalamus Part of the brain involved in regulating involuntary functions, such as body temperature.

Imaging techniques Technologies that allow visualization of internal organs using special instruments.

Marijuana Illegal drug from the plant *Cannabis sativa*.

Melatonin Chemical produced by the brain that regulates wakefulness.

Meninges Special protective membranes that enclose the brain and spinal cord.

Motor cortex Brain area involved in controlling voluntary movements.

Motor nerves Neurons that carry information from the spinal cord to the muscles.

Myelin White, fatty material that insulates some axons.

Nerve A cordlike bundle of fibers made of nerve cells or neurons that transmits electric messages through the body.

Nerve impulse Electrical signal transmitted by neurons.

Neuron Cell of the nervous system specialized for transmitting electrical signals throughout the body.

Neurotransmitter A chemical released by a neuron that relays information to the next neuron.

Neural Related to the nervous system.

Nociceptors Nerve endings that signal the sensation of pain.

Olfactory cortex Area of the brain involved in sensing smells.

Papillae Small, round bumps on the top of the tongue that contain taste buds.

Parietal cortex Area of the brain, located on the left and right sides, involved in visual and spatial tasks, and in the sense of touch.

Parosmia Malfunction of the sense of smell that causes harmless or pleasant odors to be perceived as offensive.

Peripheral nervous system (PNS) Nerves outside of the brain and spinal cord.

Phantosmia Malfunction of the sense of smell that causes sensation of odors that are not present.

Reflex Involuntary action or response, such as the knee jerk response, that does not involve the brain.

Sense Ability to receive and perceive inside or outside signals, like hearing, sight, sound, smell, and touch.

Sensory cortex Areas of the brain specialized in processing external signals perceived by the senses.

Sensory nerves Neurons that carry signals from the senses to the brain and spinal cord.

Spinal column Bony canal that houses the spinal cord.

Spinal cord Thick, whitish cord of nerves that runs from the bottom of the brain inside the spinal column.

Sulci Narrow grooves separating adjacent convolutions of the brain.

Synapse A gap between two neurons where chemical signals travel from one neuron to another.

Visual cortex Area of the brain specialized in processing images coming from the eyes.

Ventricles Spaces inside the brain filled with cerebrospinal fluid.

Wernicke's area Brain region responsible for the comprehension of language.

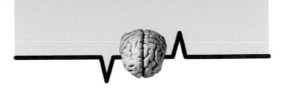

Bibliography

ABS Education Alliance. "New Technologies that Help Control Your Vehicle." *ABS Education Alliance.* Available online. URL: http://www.abs-education.org/ishs/techindex.html.

Alters, Sandra. *Biology: Understanding Life.* Sudbury, Mass.: Jones and Bartlett Publishers, 2000

Bower, Bruce. "Sleepyheads' Brains Veer from Restful Path." *Science News* 157:7 (2000): 103.

Bower, James, and Lawrence Parsons. "Rethinking the 'Lesser Brain.'" *Scientific American* (August 2003): 50–57.

Chudler, Eric H. *Neuroscience for Kids.* Available online. URL: http://faculty.washington.edu/chudler/neurok.html.

Dehaene, S., et al. "Sources of Mathematical Thinking: Behavioral and Brain-imaging Evidence." *Science* 284 (1999): 970–974.

Dietrich, A., and W.F. McDaniel. "Endocannabinoids and Exercise." *British Journal of Sports Medicine* 38 (2004): 536–541.

Drummond, S.P.A. "Altered Brain Response to Verbal Learning Following Sleep Deprivation." *Nature* 403 (2000): 655.

———. "Sleep Deprivation-induced Reduction in Cortical Functional Response to Serial Subtraction." *NeuroReport* 10 (1999): 3745.

Eliot, Lise. *What's Going On In There? How the Brain and Mind Develop in the First Five Years of Life.* New York: Bantam Books, 1999.

Ezzell, Carol. "Brain Terrain: Mapping the Functions of Various Areas of the Human Brain is Difficult—and Controversial." *Scientific American* (March 2000): 22–23.

Field, Tiffany. *Touch.* Cambridge, Mass.: MIT Press, 2001.

Gage, Fred. "Repair Yourself: How Do You Fix a Broken Brain?" *Scientific American* (September 2003): 46–53.

Greenfield, Susan. *The Human Mind Explained*. New York: Henry Holt, 1996.

Gross, Charles. *Brain, Vision, and Memory: Tales in the History of Neuroscience*. Cambridge, Mass.: MIT Press, 1998.

Harris, Christine. "The Mystery of the Ticklish Laughter." *American Scientist* 87 (1999): 344.

Healy, Jane. *Your Child's Growing Mind: Brain Development and Learning from Birth to Adolescence*. New York: Broadway Books, 2004.

Holloway, Marguerite. "The Mutable Brain. Score One for Believers in the Adage 'Use it or Lose It.'" *Scientific American* (September 2003): 78–85.

Howard, Pierce. *The Owner's Manual for the Brain: Everyday Applications from Mind-Brain Research*. Austin, Tex.: Bard Press, 2000.

Johnson, Steven. *Mind Wide Open: Your Brain and the Neuroscience of Everyday Life*. New York: Scribner, 2004.

Klawans, Harold. *Why Michael Couldn't Hit and Other Tales of the Neurology of Sports*. New York: Avon Books, 1996.

Klösch, Gerhard, and Ulrich Kraft. "Sweet Dreams are Made of This." *Scientific American MIND* (June 2005).

Krogh, David. *Biology: A Guide to the Natural World*. New York: Pearson–Prentice Hall, 2005.

Lyamin, Oleg, et al. "Continuous Activity in Cetaceans after Birth. The Exceptional Wakefulness of Newborn Whales and Dolphins Has No Ill-effect on their Development." *Nature* 435 (2005): 1177.

Murray, Bridget. "From Brain Scan to Lesson Plan." *Monitor on Psychology* 31:3 (March 2000). Available online. URL: http://www.apa.org/monitor/mar00/brainscan.html.

Pica, Pierre, et al. "Exact and Approximate Arithmetic in an Amazonian Indigene Group." *Science* 306 (2004): 499–503.

Ramachandran, V.S., and Sandra Blakeslee. *Phantoms in the Brain: Probing the Mysteries of the Human Mind*. New York: William Morrow, 1998.

Ratey, John. *A User's Guide to the Brain: Perception, Attention, and the Four Theatres of the Brain*. New York: Pantheon Books, 2001.

Scheffler, Bjorn, et al. "Phenotypic and Functional Characterization of Adult Brain Neuropoiesis." *Proceedings of the National Academy of Sciences, USA* 102:26 (2005): 9353–9358.

Sheslow, David. "Being Afraid." *KidsHealth* (August 2004). Available online. URL: http://kidshealth.org.

Society for Neuroscience. *Brain Facts: A Primer on the Brain and Nervous System*. Washington, D.C.: Society for Neuroscience, 2005.

Springer, Sally, and Georg Deutsch. *Left Brain, Right Brain*. New York: W.H. Freeman, 1993.

Talukder, Gargi. "How the Brain Learns a Second Language." *Brain Connection* (January 2001). Available online. URL: http://www. brainconnection.com/topics/?main=fa/second-language.

Thompson, R.S., et al. "A Case-control Study of the Effectiveness of Bicycle Safety Helmets." *New England Journal of Medicine* 320 (1989): 1361–1367.

Travis, John. "Comfortably Numb: Anesthetics are Slowly Giving Up the Secrets of How They Work." *Science News Online* 166:1 (July 3, 2004). Available online. URL: http://www.sciencenews.org/articles/20040703/bob8.asp.

Viegas, Jennifer. "Scientists Grow Brain Cells in a Dish." *Discovery. com* (June 13, 2005). Available online. URL: http://dsc.discovery.com/news/briefs/20050613/brain.html.

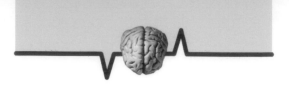

Further Reading

Ballard, Carol. *The Brain and the Nervous System*. New York: Franklin Watts, 2005.

Farndon, John. *The Big Book of the Brain: All About the Body's Control Center*. New York: Peter Bedrick Books, 2000.

Newquist, H.P. *The Great Brain Book: An Inside Look at the Inside of Your Head*. New York: Scholastic, 2005.

Simon, Seymour. *The Brain*. New York: Harper Trophy, 1999.

WEB SITES

Brain Connection: A Web Resource from Scientific Learning
http://www.brainconnection.com

Health for Kids
http://kidshealth.org/index.html

Mayo Clinic, *Brain and Nervous System Center*
http://www.mayoclinic.com/health/brain/BN00033

Museum of Science, *The Brain*
http://www.sciencemuseum.org.uk/exhibitions/brain/

Neuroscience for Kids
http://faculty.washington.edu/chudler/neurok.html

Society for Neuroscience
http://www.sfn.org

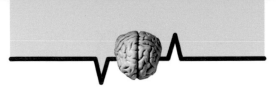

Picture Credits

page:

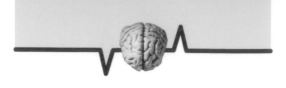

Index

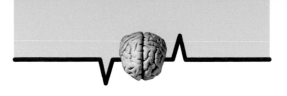

About the Author

Ana María Rodríguez, Ph.D., has been doing research in immunology and other biological and medical sciences for more than 20 years. She is currently a full-time writer, with more than 75 magazine articles published for children and adults in the areas of science, nature, medicine, health, sports, diseases, and history. She is also the author of four children's books (http://www.anamariarodriguez.com). She lives in Houston, Texas, with her husband and two sons.

ABOUT THE EDITOR

Eric H. Chudler, Ph.D., is a research neuroscientist who has investigated the brain mechanisms of pain and nociception since 1978. Dr. Chudler received his Ph.D. from the Department of Psychology at the University of Washington in Seattle. He has worked at the National Institutes of Health and directed a laboratory in the neurosurgery department at Massachusetts General Hospital. Between 1991 and 2006, Dr. Chudler was a faculty member in the Department of Anesthesiology at the University of Washington. He is currently a research associate professor in the University of Washington Department of Bioengineering and director of education and outreach at University of Washington Engineered Biomaterials. Dr. Chudler's research interests focus on how areas of the central nervous system (cerebral cortex and basal ganglia) process information related to pain. He has also worked with other neuroscientists and teachers to develop educational materials to help students learn about the brain. Find out more about Dr. Chudler and the fascinating world of neuroscience by visiting his Web site, Neuroscience for Kids, at http://faculty.washington.edu/chudler/neurok.html.